# THE CLASSICAL ASSOCIATION
## *of the* MIDDLE WESTAND SOUTH
### A History of the First Eighty Years

BY HERBERT W. BENARIO
*Professor Emeritus of Classics*

Emory University

The Classical Association
of the Middle West and South
Greenville, South Carolina
1989

The Classical Association
of the Middle West and South

Greenville, South Carolina

# THE CLASSICAL ASSOCIATION
## *of the* MIDDLE WEST AND SOUTH
### *A History of the First Eighty Years*

# Praefatio

AN AGE OF MORE THAN FOURSCORE YEARS is a grand achievement for both individual and organization. The Classical Association of the Middle West and South has now reached that stage of its existence; the time seemed suitable to undertake its history, while there were still some *seniores* whose experiences stretched back to the first decades of the Association's activities. *Memoria hominum* is particularly crucial in this enterprise, because the Association's records survive only intermittently and are by no means as full as one would wish. Much in the early years was published in *Classical Journal,* which has been an essential resource. I have examined every issue of *CJ*, and have, consequently, given a broad conspectus of the Association's, and the classical profession's, activities and concerns since the first years of this century. The choice of material for inclusion in this narrative was, of course, mine, but I hope that I have not failed to include any important subject or movement. I have frequently quoted substantial excerpts from *CJ* or the Association's records in order to give a sense of the substance and style of other eras; I preferred to have other people speak rather than to offer a paraphrase.

I am grateful to Professors Grace L. Beede, Clarence A. Forbes, John N. Hough, Gareth L. Schmeling, Graves H. Thompson, and particularly Ward W. Briggs, Jr., for information, advice, and amendment. This history is the better for their assistance; shortcomings in judgment or precision rest with me. I am also grateful to Mrs. JoAnn Pulliam, of the University of Georgia Classics Department, for skillful preparation of the final manuscript.

Herbert W. Benario

Atlanta, Georgia
December 1988

# O N E *The Foundation*

*Clarorum virorum facta moresque posteris tradere, antiquitus usitatum, ne nostris quidem temporibus quamquam incuriosa suorum aetas omisit,....*

TACITUS, *Agricola* 1.1

SO THE GREAT ROMAN HISTORIAN began his first literary work. As we approach the last decade of the twentieth century, an era which happily may be called *curiosa suorum aetas*, the present writer's purpose is the same, *si parvis componere magna licet*, with, however, one large difference. Our subject is not the nature and achievements of an individual but of an organization.

The origins of the organization which became the Classical Association of the Middle West and South cannot be understood without some background of the development of classical studies in the United States.[1] The nineteenth century falls into two parts, marked by the approach of the amateur on the one hand and of the professionally trained scholar on the other. The earlier period, beginning in 1815, boasts of the names of Bancroft and Ticknor and Everett[2] and may be said to conclude with the tenure of Harvard's chair of Greek by Cornelius Felton (1860).[3] The later period introduces German scholarship to our shores, in the figures of Whitney, Lane, Gildersleeve,[4] and Goodwin, Felton's successor, who went off to study at the feet of great men in great universities equipped with great libraries. These men, who proved to be only the first of a seeming flood, transformed the study and teaching of classical philology. They, particularly Gildersleeve, introduced the German *Seminar* to the advanced stages of instruction and began to produce scholarly works as well as to absorb them. The number of such men, which had begun to grow before the Civil War, continued to increase steadily in the years after, as one German-trained generation sent another off to Germany. The American Oriental Society included classicists among its members, but the need for an organization which could unite men of classical interests became apparent to some individuals. The result was the establishment of the American Philological Association in 1869.[5]

The professionalization of classical studies continued with the introduction of graduate study on the German model, the establishment of new universities whose purpose in education was different from that hitherto known, such as The Johns Hopkins University, Leland Stanford Jr. University, Cornell University, and the University of Chicago, and the inauguration in 1880 of *The American Journal of Philology*, edited by Gildersleeve, which appeared more frequently than the *Transactions of the American Philological Association* and was not devoted exclusively to conference papers.

Classics at the college and university levels flourished in the last decade of the nineteenth century and the first of the twentieth, but education at the lower levels faced considerable ferment from the publications of John Dewey. Secondary school teachers, often ill-trained to teach Latin, now had to concern themselves with questions of how to teach as well as to master their subject.

Numerous states had educational organizations with sections devoted to the classics where they could meet, but there was essentially no place for them in the APA, which, further, proved to be largely an organization focused upon the northeastern part of the United States. In the first forty years of its existence, the Association held its annual meeting west of Pittsburgh or south of Washington, D.C., only six times: Cleveland in 1881, Charlottesville in 1892, Chicago in 1893, Madison in 1900, St. Louis in 1904, and Chicago in 1907. Moreover, within that same period only eight men from institutions outside the northeast quadrant were elected president of the Association, three from the University of Michigan, two from the University of Virginia, and one each from the University of Chicago, Western Reserve University, and the University of Wisconsin.[6] There was, clearly, a large clientele throughout the country who required more from a professional organization than the American Philological Association was offering them, or could offer them.

In 1894, Francis W. Kelsey published an article entitled "Latin in the High School."[7] To improve the abilities of the teacher in his subject and as a pedagogue, Kelsey proposed three remedies, of which the first is absolutely essential to further progress, the other two will be powerful allies in gaining the results aimed at. They are, respectively:

> A higher standard of qualification for those who shall hereafter enter upon the work;
> A strengthening and broadening of Latin scholarship by conferences at stated periods; and
> A publication devoted to the interests of Latin and Greek in the preparatory and high schools.[8]

Kelsey did not urge the establishment of an organization which would bring together the classicists of several states or a wider region. He had in mind state conferences, and, indeed, was able to announce that such a gathering would take place in Ann Arbor in spring 1895.[9] The journal for which he found a need would not rival *AJP* or the APA's own *Transactions and Proceedings*, but "should have for its mission the promotion of the interests of Latin and Greek in the high schools and academies."[10] But Kelsey's optimism that there was no "practical difficulty" in establishing state conferences and a journal was not fully satisfied for another decade.[11]

The year 1904 was a momentous one for the city of St. Louis. It saw the Louisiana Purchase Exposition and the Third Olympic Games of the modern era, which embraced a wider array of events than any other and ran almost without a break from May through November. It also was the venue of the American Philological Association's westernmost meeting, which occurred September 16 to 19. We do not know what occurred at that meeting, whether, indeed, the very fact of a large classical convention in the heartland of the country served as the stimulus, but not long afterward, on November 1, the Classical Division of the University of Missouri at Columbia sent a letter, signed by W.G. Manly, chairman, and E.H. Sturtevant, secretary, to a wide audience. This letter, the text of which follows, was the impetus for establishment of the Classical Association of the Middle West and South.

Dear Sir:

It has seemed to a large number of men that the interests of classical study in the middle west would be promoted by an association of the classical teachers of that region. If such an organization should hold annual meetings at some central point—such as Chicago or St. Louis—it would draw a large attendance from all the states between Ohio and Colorado. Many of the teachers in high schools and small colleges who now never attend any kind of a classical meeting would undertake the journey to one of the cities just mentioned.

The Classical Division of the University of Missouri is anxious to see this idea put into effect. We are therefore addressing the teachers in the more important universities of the region in reference to the matter. Will you kindly send to one of the undersigned a reply to the following questions? Please add any suggestions that occur to you.

1. Is it your opinion that a classical association of the Mississippi valley can with profit be organized at this time?

2. For the purpose of effecting such an organization, would you be willing to attend a meeting in St. Louis during the first week—"convocation" week—of January, 1905?

3. How general should the invitation to this meeting be made?

Very truly yours,

The letter received an enthusiastic response, with more than 600 replies. Consequently, on March 11, 1905, Professor Manly distributed a formal invitation, which began as follows:

Early last November a letter was sent out by the Classical Department of the University of Missouri, inquiring whether the time was not ripe for the organization of a Classical Association in the middle West and South. It was thought that such an association, drawing upon the immense body of classical teachers living in this territory, might well bring together annually a large number of workers, and be made to promote greatly the cause to which they are devoted, not only through the holding of formal sessions with papers and discussions, but also through the hardly less valuable renewal of personal acquaintanceship, and the making of new acquaintances, based upon common interests, sympathies, and educational convictions.

The marked interest shown by the large number of favorable replies received made it seem best to organize without further delay. A meeting will accordingly be held in Chicago, on the grounds of the University, on Friday and Saturday the 5th and 6th of May.

This communication was signed by sixty-three persons from twenty-two states, with three from each state save the Dakotas; there was one representative from North Dakota while South Dakota had two. These twenty-two states represented the true heartland of the United States, reaching from the Canadian border to the Mexican and stretching east and west from the

Mississippi River. The most conspicuous absences were the Atlantic coast states, Virginia, North Carolina, South Carolina, Georgia, and Florida. Similarly, three of the westernmost members of the later Association were not present: New Mexico, Utah, and Wyoming. Nor were any Canadian provinces included. Nonetheless, the number of individual responses, greater than the membership of the American Philological Association,[12] showed that there was a need for an organization closer to home for a large part of the country and perhaps more suited to their requirements.

The response to this call was equally general and encouraging. Within days a formal invitation and copy of the program followed:

ANNOUNCEMENT
of the
CONFERENCE OF CLASSICAL TEACHERS
of the
MIDDLE WEST AND SOUTH.

*To be held in Chicago, Friday and Saturday, May 5 and 6, 1905,*
To Effect a Permanent Organization.

. . . . . . . . . . . . . . . . .

THE PURPOSE OF THE CONFERENCE

The Conference herein announced is to be held for the purpose of effecting an organization of the classical teachers of the Middle West and South, in accordance with the circular of invitation sent out from Columbia, Mo., on March 11 by Professor Manly and a number of colleagues representing the twenty-two states in the region defined. The responses to this circular have been unexpectedly large (over 600), and indicate a wide-spread feeling of the need of a closer cooperation. All questions pertaining to the permanent organization of such a body —name, scope and aims, place and time of meetings, etc.—will be discussed and determined at the meeting to be held in Chicago on May 5 and 6 next, Friday and Saturday.

The conference began with an organizational meeting, at which four committees were appointed: Constitution, Nomination of Officers, Program, and Publications. There then followed ten papers spread over four sessions; among those participating were Carl Darling Buck of the University of Chicago, John A. Scott of Northwestern University, William Gardner Hale of the University of Chicago, Gordon J. Laing of the University of Chicago, and Francis W. Kelsey of the University of Michigan. The Friday evening address was delivered by Paul Shorey of the University of Chicago, on the subject "Philology and Classical Philology."[13] One hundred eighty-three people registered, with numbers of others, including Professor Manly, failing to inscribe their names. We may well surmise that some two hundred were present for the birth of the new organization.

The actual moment of birth came after Professor Shorey's address, when the various committees which had been appointed that morning reported. The constitution presented by George L. Hendrickson of the University of Chicago had, as article 1. Name and Object of the Association,

> This organization shall be known as the Classical Association of the Middle West and South. Its object shall be the advancement of classical learning, the encouragement of classical studies within the territory indicated, and the promotion of the common interests of its members through its meetings and publications.

With approval of the constitution, the organization came to official life.

The report of the Committee on Program, presented by Frank F. Abbott of the University of Chicago, emphasized the need for papers of interest to the full range of the membership.

> The committee recommends that both articles of investigation and papers primarily of interest to the teachers as such be presented. The majority of the committee is of the opinion that approximately two-thirds of the papers should be of a technical character, and one-third should be for the teacher.

The Committee on Nomination of Officers presented its slate, with W. G. Manly proposed as president and vice-presidents named for each of the states, as well as one for the "Indian Territory."

The report of the Committee on Publications began with what may be called a given, that the Association should publish a journal "devoted to the common interests of the members, consisting of articles, reviews, notes, and editorials likely to appeal to teachers in schools, colleges and universities" and that this publication should be entitled *The Classical Journal.* The large question dealt with finance: should a fund be raised from individuals to ensure publication, or should an offer be accepted which had been tendered by the University of Chicago. The former alternative seemed difficult of achievement, the latter would place the Association deeply under obligation to one institution. Nonetheless, the Committee recommended acceptance of Chicago's offer. The report follows in full, since its implementation was crucial in the *Journal's* successful beginnings. Had its chief organ failed or been mediocre, the Association might well have faded away.

> 1. The University of Chicago has decided to publish a journal entitled Classical Philology, which is to be devoted to research in the field of Classical Studies. It will be issued quarterly, each number to consist of 96 pages or more.
> *Note:* The University intends to invite the cooperation of a number of representative scholars in various parts of the country.
> 2. In case the Classical Association of the Middle West and South should desire to undertake the publication of a Journal, and should wish a financial guarantee, the University will be glad to help in any plan that should be satisfactory to all parties concerned. The following are tentative propositions.

3. The Journal of the Association shall bear upon the title page the words "Published under the Auspices of the Classical Association of the Middle West and South," or some equivalent.

There shall be two managing editors, one of whom shall be a member of the University of Chicago.

There shall also be, in cooperation with the managing editors, a board of editors or associate editors, to be appointed by the Ex. Com. of the Association.

4. Of this journal 8 numbers of at least 24 pages each, shall be published annually, (appearing in the months of the academic year in which the other journal does not appear).

5. The field of this journal shall be the obvious common interests of the members. The material published (articles, reviews, notes, editorials, communications, and so forth) shall be of a character to appeal primarily to the teacher as such, in school or college.

It is intended that the two journals shall supplement each other, neither encroaching upon the other's field.

6. The Journal of the Association shall be entered in the Post Office department as a distinct journal.

7. The Journal of the Association and the journal entitled Classical Philology shall be sent to each member of the Classical Association.

8. The relations of the Journal of the Association and of the Journal entitled Classical Philology shall be as follows:

A. The Association shall pay to the University of Chicago the sum of $1.50 from the yearly dues of each member.

B. The University of Chicago shall be responsible for the entire expense of the Journal of the Association beyond the amount of such receipts, except as expressly provided below.

C. The University of Chicago shall receive no subscriptions from persons within the territory of the Association, except through the Treasurer of the Association; but it shall be at liberty to solicit and receive subscriptions from persons outside of this territory, and from libraries, schools and colleges within or without the territory.

D. The University of Chicago shall not offer the Journal of the Association for separate sale at a price below $2.00.

E. The University of Chicago shall bear the expenses incurred by the managing editors for postage and stationery.

F. Extra copies of the two Journals, desired for purposes of promotion, shall be furnished to the Association by the University at cost, proper notice of the order for a given issue having been furnished in advance.

G. The University of Chicago shall bear the expense of the promotion of the Journal of the Association outside the territory of the Association.

H. The University of Chicago agrees to send the Journal entitled Classical Philology to every member of the Association, without extra charge.

9. The above proposals, so far as concerns the Association, shall be incorporated in a contract valid for five years. But the contract shall not be binding until the paid membership of the Association shall reach six hundred.

The most significant parts of this proposal were that the University would assist in financing, that the material would chiefly interest the teacher, and that a contract would not be legally binding until the Association's paid membership reached 600. In the event, negotiations with the University of Chicago Press proved difficult, with problems that at first seemed insurmountable.

A memo in the Association's files, undated and unsigned, which, however, I think must be from Professor Manly and written prior to September 7, 1905, found the Press' proposal unacceptable for three reasons: the University refused to pay even one half of the expense of the prospectus for the *Journal*, it demanded a personal guarantee for the $900 before issuing the first number, and it claimed that all advertising space, and thus all advertising revenue, belonged to it. Further, the cost estimates indicated that eight issues of thirty-two pages each would cost less than the guaranteed sum. Nonetheless, the writer offered to sign a contract on the Association's behalf for a period of two years rather than five. This offer was refused. The writer's conclusion was that "It would be fatal to the Association to enter into such a contract for a period of five years."

On September 7, the writer circulated among the members of the Executive Committee a proposal from a firm in Columbia, Missouri. "On this plan we shall get a 700 edition of a 32pp. Journal for nearly $300.00 less than the personal guarantee demanded by the University of Chicago for a 600 edition. Besides, we shall control all our receipts ourselves." However, the Executive Committee, meeting in St. Louis on October 14, accepted a contract with the University of Chicago, with one major change. CAMWS was to receive one-third of the net receipts of the advertising of both journals, with a minimum of $50.00 a year. The contract was to run for five years.

Satisfactory settlement and signing of a contract in October led to the first appearance of the new *Classical Journal* in December 1905. The first four pages were devoted to editorials, which presented manifestos, *ut ita dicam*, of both association and publication. Parts of these follow:

The lists in the office of the *Journal* show that there are more than 7,000 classical teachers in the territory of the Association. That these thousands of workers should agree in all the articles of their educational creed is not for a moment to be expected. Nor is it to be desired. There are divers means of pedagogical salvation, and it is not the purpose of the new Association to convert the stimulus that comes from frank discussion into so much friction for the wearing away of individualism. Within certain limits every teacher does his best work when following the lines that he has himself laid down. But limits, none the less, exist, and it is manifest that such a presentation of the different aspects of classical study as is provided for in the plans for the programmes of the annual meeting can not fail to have a broadening and liberalizing effect.

Yet, however our interests may vary in detail, however different our methods of teaching may be, upon one thing we are all agreed—that the Greek and Latin classics are one of the best instruments for mental training; that they form an admirable introduction to the study of literature; that they contribute largely to the framing of the student's historical perspective; that translation from Greek and Latin into English, and from English into Greek and Latin, is an agency of unique efficiency for inducing accuracy and precision in thinking and speaking; in a word, that classical studies are, in the highest sense of the terms, practical and utilitarian. Nor could there be a more opportune time than the present for stating and making good our claim. For more than a decade the aims of classical study have been misunderstood and misrepresented. Latin and Greek courses have been forced within ever narrowing limits. The cry of "impractical" has been raised, and various substitutes for the classics have been offered. In some cases the subjects substituted have been excellent in themselves, but have not been appropriate for secondary work; in others a crass pseudo-utilitarian philistinism has ruled the schools; while elsewhere the fads and fancies of misty pedagogical theorists have usurped the precious hours, which, under any rational system of education, would be given to the training of the mind. Children who have been sent to school to work have been taught to play. But there are signs that these things are passing. The cruder output of the schools under the new curriculum has not met with the approbation either of business men or of college professors. The high-school graduate is found to have mussed many subjects but to have mastered none, and there has been a reaction in favor of the stricter discipline of the classical courses. In more than one school Greek has come into its own. What has been done in these schools can be done in others, and the difficulty of the task will be enormously decreased if the efforts of individuals are supported by the influence of an Association which, its founders hope, will include every efficient teacher of the classics in the twenty three central states.

◆ ◆ ◆ ◆ ◆ ◆

But although no elaborate programme is desirable or possible, the general purpose of the *Classical Journal* can be very simply stated. It is to be a journal for the teacher, both the secondary-school man and the college professor. It will not neglect the practical problems which arise daily in the work of the classroom. Yet it is the belief of the editors that we teachers of the classics in every grade need something more and better than a knowledge of method. To keep in touch with that research which is constantly throwing new light even on the Latin and Greek classics; to keep the mind alert in work that has so often proved a dry routine; to become more familiar both with the material environment of classical authors and with the social and intellectual influences under which they wrote; to bring the truth and beauty of that past into the life of today—a journal which will help the classical teacher in such aims as these would make the Association a real and vital force.[14]

Establishment of the Association was the culmination of an idea whose time had come. Morale among classicists improved as regional organizations came into being, CAMWS being only the first. The Classical Association of New England (CANE) followed the next year, the Classical Association of the Middle States and Maryland, which later changed its name to the Classical Association of the Atlantic States (CAAS), in 1907, the Classical Association of the Pacific Northwest (CAPN) in 1911, and the Classical Association of the Pacific States (CAPS) in 1915.[15] The New Englanders chose not to establish their own publication, instead benefiting from the already existing *CJ*. The Middle States, however, went their own way, with the appearance in October 1907 of the first number of *The Classical Weekly*, which announced on its first page, in a statement signed by Charles Knapp,

The object of the Classical Association of the Middle States and Maryland...is to unite all persons in the Middle States and Maryland who are interested in the study of the literature, the life, and the art of ancient Greece and ancient Rome, that the position of the Classics may be strengthened in every possible way, through the encouragement of research and the development of better methods of teaching.

Only two years after CAMWS's foundation, then, the character of the classical profession had undergone dramatic change and betterment. Where before there had been one national organization whose prime impact was in the northeast and upon college and university people, there were now three regional associations as well, whose territories embraced most of the country east of the Rockies, with the chief exception of five south Atlantic states, and whose constituencies included as many school teachers as possible. "In these later years," wrote F. G. Moore, "the whole situation has been altered by the increasing number of local organizations, which, with somewhat different aims from ours, naturally attract many of our members to meetings held at other seasons (viz. other than at Christmastime), and perhaps at more frequent intervals. Opportunity for scholarly and friendly intercourse, once limited for most of us to our yearly gatherings, are now offered by these flourishing local societies as well."[16]

The first issue of *Classical Philology* appeared in January 1906. Since the University of Chicago Press published both it and *Classical Journal* and members of CAMWS received both publications, the two were linked, perhaps unfairly, in the eyes of some of the eastern establishment. In a letter dated Nov. 2, 1905, to W.M. Lindsay, who was one of the original board of editors of CP, Basil Gildersleeve, founder and editor of *The American Journal of Philology*, wrote,

When the Chicago people told me that they were about to get up a journal of classical philology, what could I say? One man informed me that it was intended to stimulate production in the West, another that it was meant to provide a vehicle for the teeming wealth of the West, a third that it was to be largely given up to reviews of current philological literature, for which as I had often lamented, there was scant space in my Journal. Of course, they have my best wishes, but it is not in human nature to be overjoyed at an enterprise, which will certainly draw away from me valued contributors and make my editorial work harder. But as Wilamowitz wrote to me some time ago in a noble letter 'Die Wissenschaft geht vor' and I honestly wish them all success and a maintenance of the scientific standard. Some of my best friends have gone into the enterprise and your name will help them very much.

Thomas D. Seymour of Yale was not as generous. He wrote Gildersleeve on February 10: "I think my colleagues here all agree with me in regretting the establishment of *Classical Philology*, and I believe all would prefer to publish articles in your *Journal*." In reply, on February 20, Gildersleeve wrote: "The whole Chicago enterprise is a repetition of the Aaron Burr conspiracy."[17]

Does Gildersleeve refer to more than the establishment of *Classical Philology* in these comments? I do not think so; the foundation of an association which would look particularly to the advancement of teaching and of a journal with a focus so different from that of his own *American Journal of Philology* could hardly have concerned him. He certainly does not seem to have commented upon the establishment of the regional association (The Middle States and Maryland) which immediately affected him and the appearance of its publication less than two years later.[18]

## NOTES
1. See W. M. Calder III, "Die Geschichte der klassischen Philologie in den Vereinigten Staaten," *Jahrbuch für Amerikastudien* 11 (1966) 213-240 = *Studies in the Modern History of Classical Scholarship* (Naples 1984) 15-42 and G.A. Kennedy, "Afterword: An Essay on Classics in America since the Yale Report," in M. Reinhold, *Classica Americana* (Detroit 1984) 325-351.
2. See M. Reinhold, "The Silver Age of Classical Studies in America, 1790-1830," in *Classica Americana* (above, n. 1) 174-203 and "'A New Morning': Edward Everett's Contributions to Classical Learning," *ibid* 204-213.
3. See D. Wiesen, "Cornelius Felton and the Flowering of Classics in New England," CO 59 (1981-82) 44-48.
4. See W.W. Briggs, Jr., and H.W. Benario, eds., *Basil Lanneau Gildersleeve* (Baltimore 1986); Briggs, *The Letters of Basil Lanneau Gildersleeve* (Baltimore 1987); and P. Shorey, "Fifty Years of Classical Studies in America," TAPA 50 (1919) 33-61.

5. See F. G. Moore, "A History of the American Philological Association," *TAPA* 50 (1919) 5-32 and L. R. Shero, *The American Philological Association. An Historical Sketch* (Philadelphia 1964).
6. See H. Bloch's Supplement to the *Index of the Transactions and Proceedings of the American Philological Association Volumes 1-100, 1870-1969* 327-337.
7. *Educational Review* 8 (1894) 25-42.
8. *ibid* 31.
9. *ibid* 39-41. Kelsey had arranged this meeting: *Nat. Cyclop. of American Biography* 26 (1937) 461-462.
10. *ibid* 41.
11. *ibid* 42.
12. In June 1902, APA had 471 members: E. Sihler, "Klassische Studien und Klassischer Unterricht in den Vereinigten Staaten," *Neue Jahrbücher für das klassische Altertum, Geschichte und deutsche Literatur und für Pädagogik* 10 (1902) 515. In 1905 this figure had risen to 578: *TAPA* 36 (1905) xcix.
13. *CJ* 1 (1905-06) 169-196.
14. *ibid* 2-4.
15. W. Agard, "Classical Scholarship," in M. Curti, *American Scholarship in the twentieth century* (Cambridge, MA, 1953) 162; *CJ* 7 (1911-12) 2.
16. Moore (above, n. 5) 26.
17. Briggs (above, n. 4) 266-268. Since members of CAMWS received both CJ and CP for $1.50 of dues, while each cost $2.00 separately, CP was able to begin its existence with a substantial subscription list, largely different from that of AJP, and was therefore spared competition with the latter.
18. For brief treatment of the events of this chapter see W.L. Carr, "Our Association—The First Fifty Years," *CJ* 50 (1954-55) 195-196.

# T W O  *The First Decade*

FROM ITS BEGINNING, CAMWS has had to face continually two important challenges, the first logistical, that of survival and growth, the second educational and philosophical: what is to be the relationship of classicists on the college/ university level and those who teach in secondary schools, both on the program of the annual meeting and in choice of material for the *Journal*. Without the strength of an adequate membership no organization can survive, and so the early years looked to reaching all classicists in the Association's region until a "satisfactory" number of members was attained.

Since negotiations for the publication of CJ were not concluded until mid-October, the first number did not appear until December; it was followed by six more on a monthly basis, making a total of seven for the year rather than the contractual eight. But the issues were much larger than the publishing contract specified, which spoke of eight issues of at least twenty-four pages each. The first four issues of volume one offered thirty-two pages, the next two forty, and the seventh forty-four. The total was thus 252 pages rather than a minimum of 192. It was a good beginning for the second major classical periodical in the United States, following *The American Journal of Philology* by a bit more than a quarter of a century and preceding *Classical Philology* by one month.

One of the *Journal's* goals was to inform the classical community of events, trends, and ideas. In the first issue, therefore, considerable space was devoted to the announcement of a department entitled "Reports from the Classical Field." The statement was signed by J.J. Schlicher of Terre Haute, Indiana.

> As the representative of a large body of classical teachers, the *Classical Journal* considers it a duty to keep them in touch with one another, and to make them acquainted with the varying conditions under which the work of classical instruction is done, with the goals that are set up, and the means that are employed to reach them.
>
> Classical teachers, like other people, can not live by bread, nor yet by highly technical articles, alone. In particular, that great number of them who, in high schools, normal schools, and small colleges, must perform their work at a distance from universities and libraries, are in constant need of a means of communication between themselves and the larger world of workers in their field. Scholarship, original production, and effective teaching are possible under very adverse circumstances; but for a normal, healthy growth they need the interest and sympathy of fellow-workers, the feeling of ideals held in common, the clearer vision that comes from an acquaintance with other conditions than one's own, and the inspiration that is given by a knowledge of efforts and struggles by others working along the same line.
>
> As things are at present, there is practically no opportunity for the average teacher in an isolated position to keep himself informed of what is going on. It is not surprising if many a classical student of good promise goes out from the university with high resolutions, and in a very

few years comes to an end, both as a scholar and as a teacher worthy of the name, from sheer starvation. It is not only as one of the *Journal's* duties, therefore, but as an effort to supply an urgent need, that the editors have decided to set apart several pages each month for "Reports from the Classical Field."

It will not be amiss to indicate in detail some of the lines along which information may be mutually helpful:

1. Existing conditions and changes in the organization of school systems and in the courses of study; requirements for entrance and graduation in the various institutions, so far as they affect the classics; statistics of attendance in Latin and Greek classes, as compared with that in other subjects; establishment of professorships and fellowships, and appointments to important positions in schools and colleges, and to other positions connected with classical work.

2. Important lines of study and investigation undertaken in university courses and seminars, or by individuals; publications planned or in progress, such as journals, studies, or doctor's dissertations; other undertakings of interest to classical teachers, e.g. expeditions, excavations, the establishment or increase of special libraries and museums, conferences, commissions, and so forth.

3. Methods and means of instructions; the material equipment for classical work in schools and colleges; the preparation of the teacher, and ways and means at his disposal for continuing the work of self-improvement when actively engaged in teaching; vacation study, travel, etc.

4. Programmes and accounts of the work of classical clubs and associations, and of organizations of teachers and pupils; accounts of the presentation of classical plays, and of other means of arousing and giving expression to an interest in classical study.

5. The most important foreign news in the classical field, so far as it can be obtained and is of interest to American teachers.

The precise lines to be followed will naturally be determined by the needs of the *Journal's* readers, and not only contributions, but questions and suggestions will be most welcome. The success of the undertaking will depend very largely on the interest which the readers take in it, and on the extent to which they are personally willing to co-operate by making contributions. It may not seem much that the individual can contribute, nor interesting to him on account of his familiarity with it, but his experience may nevertheless be different from that of others, and may present the matter from a new point of view. And if there should be absolutely nothing to report, the way is still left open to create a condition or bring to pass an event which will call for a report later on. [1]

Since the first meeting, when membership was estimated to be 600, the roll of paid-up members had risen by early 1906 to 786, divided by states as follows: Alabama 6; Arkansas 3; Colorado 8; Illinois 151; Indiana 69; Iowa 86; Kansas 29; Kentucky 10; Louisiana 4; Michigan 70; Minnesota 23; Mississippi 9;

Missouri 76; Nebraska 35; North Dakota 3; Ohio 66; Oklahoma 4; South Dakota 10; Tennessee 14; Texas 17; West Virginia 5; Wisconsin 88.[2]

The second annual meeting of the Association was in St. Louis in early May. In some respects, it was to be more important than the first, which had been concerned with foundation. This gathering had to face the questions of maintenance of life and expansion of activity; with a viable organ of publicity, the organization could exert influence in the educational field that classicists had not previously had and could perhaps help stem the assault upon the classics. The call to the St. Louis convention offered what could almost be called a platform for the organization.

> But apart from these considerations there are special reasons why every member of the Association should endeavor to attend this meeting. Coming as it does at the end of the first year of the Association's activity, it gives us an opportunity of considering in detail the many questions that have arisen in the course of these months. We can take stock, and lay our plans for the future in the light of past experience. We must, for example, devise ways and means of increasing our membership. To be sure, our growth in a single year has been remarkable. It has been amply demonstrated that ours is a real and not an artificial union; we have now nearly nine hundred members in good standing. But the work has only begun. There are thousands of classical teachers in the territory whom we have not yet reached—men and women whose co-operation is as essential to our complete success as it is to their own academic efficiency; and it is only at a large and representative meeting that we can determine upon the best methods of interesting them in the cause. There are other questions also which should receive careful consideration: What relations can be established between our Association and the various local classical conferences? That there is an opportunity here for mutual strengthening can hardly be doubted. Again, in what way can the Association best bring its influence to bear upon the making of school and college curricula? The representatives of other organizations and other departments have for a long time been persistently pushing their subjects to the front. Their influence upon boards of trustees, school superintendents, and college faculties has been enormous. Subjects to which, ten years ago, little time was given, and subjects entirely new, have shown an astounding and in some cases deplorable expansion. This has invariably resulted in the crowding, or even the exclusion, of studies of the older curriculum, among which the classics have suffered most severely. The Association would fail in one of its most important functions if it did not meet the situation resolutely and combat what its members must regard as dangerous influences in modern educational theory.[3]

In the event, two hundred members attended the meeting. The program had been arranged by invitation, and for the future two innovations were voted.

The printed program would contain not only the title of the paper and the author's name but also a brief statement of the paper's thesis or argument and one or two members would be appointed to lead the discussion of each paper. "The proposed arrangement entails a cutting-down of the number of papers, and that too seems to us desirable."[4] In spite of this noble and almost Draconian measure, the desired discussion seldom ensued.

The final number of CJ's second volume reported that satisfactory negotiations with the New England Classical Association had been completed. The latter had opted against establishing a journal of its own. Henceforth the two Associations would cooperate, the New Englanders furnishing an Associate Editor to the Editorial Board.

The third year of the Association's existence continued to focus upon greater involvement of more people in activities furthering the classical cause and in increasing discussion of papers at the annual meeting. Special committees of ten or more were organized in each of the twenty-two member states. These committees, chaired by the state vice-president, were intended to be permanent parts of the organization; they were expected to strengthen the Association's work at the local level. The Program Committee decided that brief abstracts of the papers to be presented at the spring meeting would be published beforehand in the *Journal*. And the year saw the first expansion of the Association's territory.

The Association at its founding was essentially a grouping of states centered upon the Mississippi River, actually more Middle West than South. In 1908 the missing southern Atlantic states were admitted to membership, as was an upper northwestern state: Virginia, North Carolina, South Carolina, Georgia, Florida, and Idaho increased the number of states to twenty-eight. The shape of the Association had now almost reached its final form. Both by this accession of new territory and continued growth, the membership of CAMWS rose above 1500, to reach 1700 in 1909.

For the first time, the annual meeting was held in a city other than Chicago or St. Louis. The choice was the "Athens of the South," Nashville. The meeting served as a test for the new program arrangements as well as to see whether southerners would support a meeting in their midst. The program as published in CJ indicated the main lines of each paper's argument and identified the discussion leader.

It is an excellent programme, representative of all interests, well balanced, and especially noticeable for the large number of papers in which the subjects are of immediate bearing on the practical work of school and college teachers. A commendable feature is the systematic arrangement made for discussion. In the case of each paper a summary of the content or line of argument is given and a leader of the discussion named. The *Journal* has always contended for fewer papers and more discussion. Even a brief discussion of five or ten minutes will often do more to drive home the essential points of a paper than twice that time spent by a reader in further elaboration of his theme. Under the admirable arrangements made by the Programme Committee, the plan will have a good trial.

We urge all members of the Association to be present. Apart from the excellence of the programme and the very attractive arrangements which Vanderbilt University and Peabody College are making for our entertainment, the meeting is an especially important one. It is the first occasion on which the Association has convened elsewhere than at Chicago or St. Louis, and upon the degree of success attained will depend very largely the future policy of the Association in regard to the place of meeting. In our opinion the advantages of going to different places outweigh the central position and the railroad facilities which are so often urged in favor of Chicago and St. Louis. To hold meetings at points on the extreme boundaries of our territory would not of course be wise, but there are a number of places, seats of universities or normal schools, with satisfactory railroad facilities and in the center of a large section of our territory, which would afford every opportunity for a successful meeting: Cincinnati, Bloomington, Ind., Urbana, Ill., Iowa City, Madison, Ann Arbor, and others. Wherever a meeting is held the local interest is intensified and there is invariably a substantial increase in the roll of members. Moreover, our territory is so large that it is only by meeting in different places that we can give all our members an equal opportunity of taking part in the programmes and in the management of the Association.[5]

The program consisted of sixteen papers and an invited address on the Friday evening. The chief business conducted at the meeting led to the appointment of a committee to help classicists "provide for the common defense" of their discipline against a variety of enemies. The relationship of smaller classical groups with the Association also received consideration. An editorial in *CJ* addressed this subject.

## THE UNIFICATION OF CLASSICAL SCHOLARSHIP

This caption does not indicate that classical scholarship is in a condition of unity, but that such unification is an end much to be desired. A general view of the history of scholarship, classical or otherwise, reveals the fact that scholars have not been sufficiently united in the interests of a common cause. There has been, on the one hand, lack of sympathy and co-operation among students in the same field, due to a too limited knowledge of each other's work, a too restricted personal acquaintance with fellow-workers, an indifference to all except one's own necessarily narrow lines of work; not to mention the open hostility often existing between those who should be active co-workers, springing from personal, institutional, and sectional misunderstanding, jealousy, and prejudice. Such a condition has been more than disastrous to the cause in which all have common and vital interest.

Classical scholars in particular have need to unite their forces and work in the closest possible understanding and sympathy; this, for the reason that the classics have in this age as never before been put upon the defensive by a materialistic generation that "seeketh after a sign," the sign of utility. Classicists have themselves to thank for much of the embarrassment in which they find themselves. To a united and organized front of opposition, they have presented a straggling and inharmonious line of defense. To a persistent demand that they stand and deliver cause why they should exist, they have had no clear-cut answer in which they could all agree.

It was with this feeling of need, and in view of the diverse opinions prevailing among classical scholars regarding the aims of classical study and the consequent embarrassment to the best concert of interests, that, at the recent conference at Nashville, the following motion, presented by Professor F. C. Eastman, of the University of Iowa, was adopted by the Association: "That a commission of seven be appointed by the Executive Committee whose duty shall be to collate and digest the leading articles of more recent years pertaining to the subject and to formulate the common aims and purposes of classical study."

It was understood that the findings of this commission should be published in the *Classical Journal* for the benefit of all teachers of the classics. In order to leave the executive committee entirely untrammeled in its choice, the personnel of this commission is not necessarily confined to members of the Classical Association of the Middle West and South.

This movement toward a common understanding, and a uniformity of aims is encouraging and should produce good results. Still more encouraging is the movement toward intelligent and sympathetic co-operation which has for several years past been in progress, the formation of classical associations in different sections of the country. These have already proved themselves of great value, presenting as they do an opportunity of extending personal acquaintance among scholars, and a means of presentation and discussion of problems and aims from the various fields of individual workers. In order still further to enhance the value of our own Classical Association, a second motion was presented at Nashville by Professor Eastman, looking toward the affiliation of smaller classical clubs and societies with the large Association. This motion, as adopted by the conference, was as follows:

Each state vice-president shall be authorized to organize in his own state an auxiliary association which shall be known as the—— section of the Classical Association of the Middle West and South, of which all members of the Classical Association shall be members *ex facto*, and whose purpose shall be primarily the consideration of local classical interests and their relation to the Association. These sections shall meet at least once a year at a place and time to be determined by the state vice-president, who shall be *ex officio* chairman. The vice-president shall transmit to the secretary-treasurer a record of such proceedings of the section as may be of general interest within four weeks following the date of the section meeting.[6]

The awareness of the importance of the expansion of classical organizations to the state and even local level continued to be a subject on the editorial pages of the *Journal*. But, early in 1909, an editorial brought another area of importance for the cause of the classics to the fore; it speaks to the 1980s as lucidly as it did to the end of the first decade of this century. It was signed by Charles D. Adams of Dartmouth College, editor for New England. It merits quotation *in extenso*.

But there is an even more important work that the local clubs should do, but which they seem in few cases to have attempted. This is the work of developing among the educated people in their communities a group of lovers of the classics. The immediate danger to classical studies is not so much the danger that they will be driven out of the schools and colleges, as that they will be shut up within them. The local classical club ought to bring together a group of college graduates who have had more or less of Latin and Greek in college, but who are losing their knowledge of both by disuse; the young physician who looks back on his academy course in Vergil as one of the most delightful experiences of his boyhood, but who never got quite to the point of reading Vergil easily and for pleasure; the lawyer who read Demosthenes on the Crown when he was a college sophomore, but who has no conception of what the great speech would mean to him if he could read it now with his mature appreciation of oratory and of politics; the minister who has Greek enough to enable him to use his New Testament commentary, but who will never read his Plato unless he has help from people who know more about Greek than he does; the young woman "at home" who felt the charm of the Greek drama in her college studies, but who will certainly never take it up again unless she has some special impulse and some real help on the linguistic side. The truth is that with the shortening of the time that the ordinary student in the classical course of our colleges is willing to give to Latin and Greek, the ordinary graduate comes out at about the point where he is prepared to begin the serious study of the literature, but where he will almost certainly drop the study unless he finds himself under some outside stimulus and among people who will give him some real assistance. These classical graduates who have never carried their studies to the point of large fruitfulness are the really dangerous enemies of classical studies; as time goes on and they realize that the ancient literatures have little or no place in their present intellectual life, they question the value of the classical training, and when their children in turn come into school, we find these parents saying that they prefer to have their time given to the modern studies. Greek studies in particular are suffering in our schools today because so many of the men and women in our communities who have studied Greek in college have dropped it without ever having carried it to a point where they had the knowledge or the maturity to appreciate it. Their knowledge of the Greek literature is that of their youth; if they could bring to it the taste and judgement of mature manhood, they would become champions of a culture in which they are now losing faith. If in any community the teacher of Greek in the school sees his classes diminishing, the most effective measure that he can take to restore interest is to gather together the group of men and women who have some knowledge of the language, and help them to come into some real appreciation of the literature.[7]

Volume five of *CJ* was marked by the attention given to the report of the Commission on College Entrance Requirements in Latin and its antecedents. The Commission had been established in 1908 by the American Philological Association, at the request of CAMWS, the Classical Association of the Atlantic States, and the Classical Association of New England. Its charge was "to formulate definitions of such requirements and to further the adoption of these definitions by our colleges and universities."[8] At the conclusion of this volume, the publishing contract with the University of Chicago expired. The University Press made the most satisfactory proposal for a new contract, under the terms of which *CJ* was entirely separate from *Classical Philology* in financial management. *CP* would continue to be furnished to members of the Association for substantially the same low cost (about thirty-eight cents a copy) as before. Further, there would subsequently be nine numbers of *CJ* each year rather than eight, without, however, an increase in the total number of pages. The first issue of a volume would henceforth appear in early October rather than November.

The Association's life had now settled into a necessary routine. A satisfactory pattern of meetings had developed, and the *Journal* had passed from birth to adolescence, as it were, with a *lustrum*. It had grown increasingly larger and the new contract was more favorable financially. The great challenges now were to maintain the momentum of influence on the classical scene and in the wider educational world. Both at the meetings and in the pages of *CJ*, there was a quality of preaching to the converted and of shipping coals to Newcastle.

At the 1911 meeting, two resolutions were introduced and passed, of general interest and importance.

## EXCAVATIONS IN ASIA MINOR

WHEREAS, The preservation of priceless monuments of history and archaeology is seriously imperiled by the rapid advancement of commercial enterprise in Asia Minor; and

WHEREAS, All that untold wealth of material for the better understanding of the civilizations represented by Babylon, Greece, Rome, and early Christianity can be saved only by immediate, continuous, and systematic exploration and excavation; be it

RESOLVED, That the Classical Association of the Middle West and South hereby expresses its approval of the splendid plans outlined by Dr. J. R. S. Sterrett of Cornell University for not only the surface exploration, but also the thorough excavation of important sites of Asia Minor, and its eager hope that some richly endowed American institution or some American citizen of wealth will come to the rescue with a subvention adequate to save from destruction that vast and wonderful material in imminent danger of being forever lost.

## UNIFORM GRAMMATICAL TERMINOLOGY

We, members of the Classical Association of the Middle West and South, assembled in St. Louis at the annual meeting for the year 1911, desire to express our cordial approval of the movement already begun by two educational bodies in America for the harmonizing of grammatical nomenclature and our strong interest in its success.

In order that the work in all its interrelations may most successfully be accomplished, we beg to request the National Education Association, the Modern Language Association, and the American Philological Association to arrange a joint committee for the study of grammatical terminology, and the framing of a consistent system; the members of this committee to be divided as evenly as possible among the three bodies, and also to represent as evenly as possible the school and college alike, provision being made at the same time for representation of the side of school superintendence.[9]

The Executive Committee proposed an amendment to the constitution, whereby the vice-president of the Association would no longer be the vice-president for his own state. It went into effect after approval at the next annual meeting.[10]

*Classical Journal* continued its detailed reporting on the labors of the Commission on College-Entrance Requirements in Latin with an article by the chairman of the Commission, John C. Kirtland, on "The Consequents of the Commission's Report." [11] The proposals for uniformity throughout the country had met with remarkable response, although by no means a unanimous one. "The assured agreement of the Latin requirements of the four great universities which admit students only by examination (Columbia, Harvard, Princeton, and Yale) is alone enough to justify the agitation."[12]

Volume seven of the *Journal* saw two innovations, the first of which was announced as the lead editorial of the new volume.

For some time past the desirability has been felt by those interested in the *Classical Journal* of the establishment of a foreign correspondence by which our readers may receive from time to time a fresh and reliable presentation of events and tendencies in England and on the Continent of interest to classical students. After a due consideration of available men, we have succeeded in securing the services of two scholars whose occasional letters from England and Germany respectively will prove of much interest and value. Our correspondent for England will be Mr. W. E. P. Pantin, of London, assistant master in St. Paul's School, member of the council of the Classical Association and secretary of its Curriculum Committee, secretary also of the Joint Committee on Grammatical Terminology. Our correspondent for Germany will be Dr. Paul Cauer,

*Provinzial-Schulrat* and professor in Münster, whose prominence and vigor as a writer and worker in the classics make his service to us a real acquisition. We hope to publish initial installments from these contributors at an early date.[13]

Later in the year the editors announced the establishment of a new department, entitled "Queries." "It is hardly necessary to say that the editors will not attempt to answer all questions from their own knowledge: they will attempt to refer to competent authorities such as need the specialists' knowledge....the editors must feel free to decide whether a question and answer will interest only an individual or may interest others."[14] This innovation appeared for the first time in the March 1912 number. Its purpose was to assist above all the individual who did not have ready access to colleagues or libraries and to ease his educational isolation.

The high point of the *Journal*'s next volume was the publication of the 1911 Report of the United States Commissioner of Education, which reported the statistics of enrollment in all high school subjects. The Report, hitherto published annually, would henceforth appear only every five years. The figures of this one, therefore, were to prove even more significant than could have been anticipated, because they were the last before the dislocations brought on by the pressures of the war years. German, for example, which had more than twice the enrollment of French, essentially disappeared from the schools.

The combined figures for public and private high schools revealed that Latin was the fifth most popular subject, behind only English Literature, Algebra, Rhetoric, and History (other than United States), with a total of 405,502 students, representing 49.59% of the total. Greek, with 10,739 students, was more than twice as important as Spanish.[15] These figures can serve as a benchmark for comparison with those of later surveys to record the vagaries of the fortunes of Latin and Greek.

Attendance at the meeting in Indianapolis was affected by floods. The most significant action was the admission of the state of Utah to the Association's membership, making a total of twenty-nine states. The membership now stood at 1,802, distributed as follows:

Alabama, 20; Arkansas, 12; Colorado, 34; Florida, 23; Illinois, 243; Georgia, 29; Idaho, 12; Indiana, 139; Iowa, 142; Kansas, 137; Kentucky, 62; Louisiana, 26; Michigan, 108; Minnesota, 70; Mississippi, 20; Missouri, 128; Nebraska, 65; North Carolina, 21; North Dakota, 22; Ohio, 200; Oklahoma, 15; South Carolina, 12; South Dakota, 19; Tennessee, 43; Texas, 52; Virginia, 35; West Virginia, 12; Wisconsin, 100.[16]

When the new contract for publication of the *Classical Journal* had been negotiated, it called for the printing of eight issues of forty-eight pages each, a total of 384 pages. With the beginning of volume six, the number of issues was increased to nine, without, however, an increase in the number of pages. The next volumes, therefore, consisted of six issues of forty-eight pages and three of thirty-two. During the course of volume nine (1913-1914), which itself had 416 pages, additional pages were authorized, to make nine issues uniformly of forty-eight pages each, a total of 432 pages.

Volume ten contained the following item:

## A BUREAU OF INFORMATION

A recent letter from one of our correspondents contained the following statement: "There seems to be no bureau of information in our Classical Association, and so I hope you will pardon my troubling you," etc. On the contrary, it should be understood that the Association's *Journal* is its bureau of information; and, while we are not planning a formal department of "Questions and Answers," we shall be glad to answer or obtain answers to pertinent questions from our readers and publish these answers in an appropriate place in the *Journal*, where the questions seem to be of more than individual interest. [17]

Clearly the establishment of the department entitled "Queries" had not been a success. It obviously did not receive either the quantity or kind of inquiry which would produce publishable material. One wonders how this new opportunity was expected to differ.

The officers of the Association continued to be concerned with pleading the case of the classics to those outside the profession.[18] As a result, the establishment of a Committee on Publicity was authorized in 1914. Its first report the following year proposed two plans.

One of the greatest newspaper syndicates of the Middle West has agreed to take for its use an unlimited number of "stories" on classical themes. These will be used in "boiler-plate," "type-high miscellany," and "patent insides." The circulation of such matter is enormous, as everyone knows. Articles submitted must possess "news interest" and be "snappy."

The second plan of the committee is intended to provide for the dissemination of matter relating more directly to the study of the classics. The editors of the *Classical Journal* have agreed to devote the last two pages of each number to an article, or a series of articles, along this line. The next to the last page of the *Journal* will contain articles furnished through the committee, and will be printed in brevier type in two columns, so that the page may be detached and used for "copy." The article in the penultimate page of this issue has already been mentioned in the *Journal*.

Every member of the Association who reads the *Journal* is requested to detach the page of "copy" and to present it personally to the editor of at least one newspaper, magazine, educational journal, or other periodical of his city or town, with the request that it be printed. Members are also asked, and urged, to furnish papers to the committee for this purpose. Material may be original or borrowed; we cannot afford to be too finical about credit for this cause. The committee will not be able to prepare all the "copy," but it will act as a clearing-house for material which members may submit.

The publicity committee was authorized because of the belief of the Association that the studies and opinions of those best fitted to appreciate the classics reach too narrow a circle when published in our technical journals. We convince ourselves, who are already convinced; a wider public remains uninstructed and uninspired. The day is past when we as lovers of the classics dare hesitate, with any sort of mock modesty, to herald the merits of our "wares." Our cause is just, and we may as well determine frankly to use the methods of advertising which have become so potent in the business world. Our "advertising" must be dignified and veracious. Indeed, the conservative commercial advertiser does not use the fog-horn; he pursues the scriptural counsel to set his light on a candlestick rather than hide it under a bushel. [19]

At the same meeting in 1915, the relationship between the Association and *Classical Philology* was severed. Members of the Association had always received the learned journal as a benefit of their membership. Many complained that the contents of CP were too esoteric and scholarly for their taste and resented the cost to the Association, which proved never to be more than forty cents per person. But that sum, though small, represented one-fifth of the membership income of the Association. Therefore, those who wished to continue to receive CP would pay an additional forty cents; this figure was substantially below the regular subscription cost. The new arrangement continued to benefit members who desired to receive the University of Chicago publication and dramatically increased the monies which the officers of the Association were able to budget.

Between the tenth and eleventh annual meetings of the Association, much of Europe had gone to war. The United States was still uninvolved and officially neutral. In the following year, President Woodrow Wilson would win reelection on the basis of the popular slogan, "He kept us out of war." That circumstance would soon change. With that change would come others, to life in general and education in particular. Opposition to the classics had existed in colonial days in the persons of such as Benjamin Franklin and Benjamin Rush, who were more concerned with the "useful." Opposition had never ceased in the decades that followed; it was now to intensify under the extraordinary pressures of war.

## NOTES

1. CJ 1 (1905-06) 21-22.
2. *ibid* 68.
3. *ibid* 129-30.
4. CJ 2 (1906-07) 281.
5. CJ 3 (1907-08) 171-172.
6. *ibid* 297-298.
7. CJ 5 (1909-10) 50-51.

8. *ibid* 155. See J.C. Kirtland, "The Antecedents of the Commission's Report," 147-154; "Report of the Commission on College Entrance Requirements in Latin," 155-160; Kirtland, "The Report of the Commission," 243-249.
9. CJ 6 (1910-11) 321-322.
10. *ibid* 322.
11. *ibid* 330-342.
12. *ibid* 341.
13. CJ 7 (1911-12) 1.
14. *ibid* 193.
15. CJ 8 (1912-13) 319.
16. *ibid* 354.
17. CJ 10 (1914-15) 194.
18. *ibid* 245.
19. *ibid* 267, 269.

# THREE *The First World War*

THE OUTBREAK OF THE WAR IN EUROPE had little direct effect upon the life of the Association. More than two years had passed before the United States became a participant. When American troops arrived in France, the stalemate of trench warfare with its enormous slaughter on both sides awaited infusions of men and materiel for resolution. As it happened, American forces and industrial might made the difference, with the armistice of November 11, 1918, at 11:00 A.M., returning peace to a world that would never be the same.

The Association continued in its pattern of annual meetings and regular appearance of *Classical Journal*. No meetings were cancelled because of exigency, publication was not hindered by a shortage of paper. But in the years following the war the educational climate was vastly different, not only in the United States but in Great Britain and on the continent. The value of study of the ancient languages and their civilizations was challenged as never before; classicists found themselves constantly on the defensive. This circumstance required bold responses.

The change in the relationship of the Association and *Classical Philology* meant that all membership income, save for the necessary expenses of running the Association, could be funneled into the publication of *CJ*. Consequently, with the beginning of volume eleven, the number of pages was again increased. There were now nine numbers of sixty-four pages each, a total of 576 for the volume. The editors also felt themselves compelled to include some scholarly articles which earlier would have found a home in *CP* and were now able to include in one number articles of substantial length which earlier had been divided into two or more issues. Yet all the Association's initiatives did not find immediate success. The Publicity Committee suffered from lack of contributions. It repeated its call for material: "Articles which show concretely and pointedly the 'practical' use of the classics ought to be especially effective. As yet scarcely any articles have been received.... We have the choice of taking our places on the firing-line or of being exterminated."[1]

The Committee had produced, within half a year from the spring meeting, its first salvo in the struggle for recognition of our subjects.

> The pamphlet authorized at Nashville is now ready. It is in the form of a dialogue of only ten pages between *filius* and *pater*, and is entitled "Arguing with Bob." Copies will be sent to all members of the Association. A first edition of 10,000 is being printed. The committee hopes that many times that number will ultimately be required. In order to finance possible future editions the nominal price for the pamphlet of one cent each, 20 cents for 25, and 70 cents a hundred will be charged. Cash must be sent with the order to the chairman of the committee, Professor C. H. Weeler, Iowa City, Iowa.

## "ARGUING WITH BOB"

The bright little pamphlet already mentioned as recently issued by our Publicity Committee represents a father enlightening his son as to the value of the study of the classics, and encouraging him to continue with his Latin. The idea is a happy one in that it brings the father into the discussion of the problem, and it is indeed the interest of the father which should be enlightened and enlisted in this cause, for it is he who ultimately decides the studies which his children are to pursue. We trust that not only every school principal and teacher, but that every father and mother will read and ponder "Arguing with Bob."[2]

The meeting in 1916 featured a distinguished visitor. The Reverend Henry Browne of University College, Dublin, president of the Classical Association of Ireland, delivered the main address on "Our Renaissance: Its Meaning, Aim, and Method."[3] Further, the states of New Mexico and Wyoming were admitted to membership in the Association, but Idaho withdrew to join the newly-formed Classical Association of the Pacific States. *Classical Journal* was adopted as the latter's official publication, and an editor for the Pacific States joined the Editorial Board.

Thus, within the span of a decade, the movement which began with CAMWS' foundation, to establish regional organizations throughout the country, reached fruition. There were four regional classical associations, which incorporated every state in the union: CAMWS, the Classical Association of the Atlantic States, the Classical Association of New England, and CAPS. The *Classical Journal* was the publication of all save CAAS, which issued *Classical Weekly*. In 1905, only the American Philological Association had brought classicists together on more than a local scale, and only the *American Journal of Philology* had existed as a means of publication of more than annual appearance. Now there were substantial regional organizations and three more publications, CJ, CP, and CW.

The Association had thus reached its ultimate extent within the United States, thirty states. These have remained members without change to the present day. Expansion in future would have to be to the north.

The business session voted once again to increase the number of pages in CJ beginning with the next volume; as many as four of the nine issues were to have an additional sixteen pages, a maximum of 640 for the whole. The printing contract with the University of Chicago Press was renewed for four years. Membership as of April 15, 1916, had reached 1,940. For the first time, a major change in the format of the annual meeting was approved. Beginning in 1917, the first session would commence Thursday at noon, the last would conclude Saturday afternoon. From now on, the meeting would stretch over three days rather than two.

Early in volume 12 there appeared, for the first time, the Treasurer's Report, so that the entire membership, indeed the entire classical profession, could be informed of the Association's financial status. [4] The annual meeting once again authorized an increase in the size of the *Journal*, each number of which would cover eighty pages, a total of 720. This was almost the largest size the *Journal* would ever reach, but it was not to come to pass for some years. A proposal was also approved that in future there be a presidential address. In the past there had been frequent evening addresses by distinguished scholars, both members and invitees, but there had been no formal occasion at which the President of the Association could address the membership on a subject which he deemed important.

Volume thirteen of the *Journal* devoted substantial space to a report on the Princeton Classical Conference. Since this gathering represented a major attempt to fight back against the attack of the enemies of classics and had significant results for the future of classical studies, I have chosen to cite an extensive portion of the report.

Although the purpose and nature of the classical conference held at Princeton University on the second of last June were clearly set forth in the press prior to the meetings, yet an erroneous impression concerning them has prevailed in many quarters. Even a large number of teachers of the classics, both in the United States and in Canada, have failed to grasp the significance of this remarkable gathering. Is there any reason for wonder, then, that the utilitarian world has been able to withhold from this conference the distinction due it because of its unique importance? It seems really necessary that a statement should be made as to just what the conference was, and what it was not.

The one theme of all the addresses was the place of classical studies in liberal education. Moreover, the addresses were one and all delivered by, and expressed the carefully formulated conviction of, a number of American citizens of national and even international distinction who by vocation are not associated with the teaching of the classics. One does not need the eyes of an Argus to see that this one circumstance alone marks the Princeton conference as something very different from all those that have been held before. Even at the risk of seeming to become for the time being a mechanical cataloguer, the writer feels that he must give the complete personnel of the *conférenciers*; otherwise its importance might fail to be fully grasped.

(There follow the names of the seventeen participants, among whom were Nicholas Murray Butler, President of Columbia University, and Roscoe Pound, Dean of the Harvard Law School.)

The conference closed with an address on "The General Value of Classical Studies" by Hon. Henry Cabot Lodge, United States senator from Massachusetts.

The list just given is, as it were, that of the dramatis personae appearing before the scenes. But what went on behind the scenes is equally, if not more, significant, and is due in large measure to the thought and activities of the same class of men who made the public deliverances. Indeed, it is to a group of prominent bankers, lawyers, and other business men that is to be given the credit of having conceived and made possible just such a conference as has been held. On the other hand, for the details of the meetings, such as the securing of the speakers, the balancing of the programs, the smooth progress of the sessions, in short, the practical engineering of the whole scheme, most of the credit is due to the enthusiasm, ingenuity, and industry of Dean West, of Princeton University. The fact that leading men of affairs, not professionally connected with the quadrangle and the classroom, are the moving forces behind this movement ought to be regarded as the most substantial encouragement that has been vouchsafed the teachers of the classics for many years. For what more convincing demonstration could we ask of the correctness of our observation and of the soundness of our contention as to what constitutes a truly liberal education? At least it permits us to say that the frequent charge against us of defending the classics through fear of losing our bread and butter and because of our incurably academic habit of thought, may be, after all, only a begging of the question and needs reconsideration.

In view of the fact that all the addresses delivered at the conference have been published in book form,[5] it is outside the scope of this paper to attempt to give their substance in detail. Rather, it seems advisable to keep within the limits of a few observations upon impressions carried away from the meetings and upon two or three arguments presented by certain speakers.

Perhaps the most damning, certainly the most boring, feature of conventions of all kinds in which participants are left free to choose their own topics is the sameness of the arguments set forth. This classical conference, on the contrary, was unique in that the addresses, while intensely unanimous in their main contention, were marked by a marvelous variety of argument. Indeed, certain of the audience who had no knowledge of the hidden machinery of the meetings went away with the idea that the topics had been carefully chosen so as to avoid overlapping, and then assigned like so many themes for classroom exercises. One auditor expressed his opinion that this playing of individual parts had all been agreed upon, as it were, in caucus. The fact is, however, that each and every speaker chose his own theme, developed it in his own way, and based his support of classical studies on his own independent observations.

◆ ◆ ◆ ◆ ◆ ◆

The limits of this report preclude discussion of the processes of reasoning by which the speakers reached their conclusions. At all events, it is clear that if these claims are true the importance of the classics is very real. Whether the student in his years of manhood becomes a politician or only an elector, he is enabled by the cultivation of his sense of the continuity of human nature to resist certain movements and tendencies by taking his stand on the sure ground that according to the experience of the race they are destined to fail or even to bring disaster. On the other hand, he can with equal confidence in his position abet certain other movements and tendencies as adapted to the needs and capacities of human nature. In short, his training in the psychology of the race will make for economy in legislative effort and improvement in legislative achievement.

In his contribution to the discussion Dean Magie[6] presented an argument in favor of classical studies which aroused no little debate after the meetings. The classicists, of course, accepted it as a concession which the natural scientist ought long ago to have recognized and granted; but many non-classicists maintained that it was put forward without sufficient qualification. The point is twofold, part protest, part claim. In the first place Dean Magie very emphatically denied that the specialists in the natural and the applied sciences have the right to appropriate the term science for their departments alone. A sense of the morality of terminology should move all scholars to set the lay world an example in speaking of linguistic science and literary science. Dean Magie's protest against this theft of terms is indeed timely. The second part of the argument is a statement of fact justifying the first part. It is to the effect that in the proper study of Greek and Latin the mind receives the same type of training that it receives in conducting experiments in the natural sciences. For example, in translating (unaided, presumably) a passage of classical literature the mind works from the known to the unknown, often laboriously, to be sure; nevertheless, when the work has been accomplished the unknown becomes the known. Repetition of the process ingrains a habit of thought and a manner of viewing the world.

If Dean Magie's statement is true, the classicist will be tempted in his enthusiastic reception of it to draw many conclusions which, while perhaps correct, might still be difficult to defend convincingly. One must employ caution in applying the principle. Nevertheless it does not seem rash to assert that a student thoroughly trained in the classics is at least not devoid of a knowledge and an appreciation of the principles of observation, experiment, and proof, which in these latter days are frequently claimed as derived only from the study of the natural sciences.[7]

Charles N. Smiley of Grinnell College had the honor of delivering the first presidential address at an annual meeting. Although some of his predecessors had spoken to the Association, Professor Smiley's appearance was the first to be designated "President's address." His subject, most timely for a gathering taking place in April 1918, was "Humanism and Democracy." This capstone of the program was followed by two informal sessions which considered the Association's relation to the war.

For the first time, the Association's membership rose above 2,000, with 2,129 recorded at the time of the annual meeting.

Dean Andrew Fleming West[8] of Princeton University, who had been the guiding spirit behind the classical conference of 1917, continued his vigorous activity in defense of the classics. During the summer of 1918, another classical conference was held in conjunction with the annual meeting of the National Education Association, the purpose of which was the establishment of an American Classical League. In July 1919, at a second conference again held in conjunction with the NEA, the American Classical League was born, with the full support of the regional associations; "we regard it not as a rival or as a thing apart, but as our own organization in whose support we all unite." [9] Dean West took the chair, and spoke in part as follows:

> Though the war is over, our warfare in the schools against the weakness that springs from ignorance and from low views of duty must be pressed more strongly than ever. Otherwise we shall lose the saving help of that powerful revival of the belief in discipline and duty, which is the greatest educational benefit of the war.
>
> We care little for the classics or any other study simply as a thing by itself. But we are here to maintain the classics because they are vitally important for the sake of our own national language (a chief bond in our national unity) and other modern tongues, because they give an unsurpassed training in sound and accurate habits of study, invaluable for every calling in life which requires intelligence, and because the classics are the only common underlying linguistic and literary bond of our western civilization. They are part of the gold standard of education.
>
> We are forming this American Classical League, therefore, to invigorate our entire higher school and college education, to insist that the best training should be everywhere available for every boy and girl who can take it, to do all we can to improve our own methods of teaching, to expose the folly of all sordid or sentimental theories, to insist that there is no education worth the name unless it involves training the mind, not for the sake of money, place, or power, but in order to develop our boys and girls to their highest mental and moral excellence, to make them masters in thought and in expression, and thus to send them out equipped for lives of the highest usefulness.
>
> We have many assaults to meet. But we stand at the salient of Verdun. Let us acquit ourselves like men.[10]

Dean West was elected president with Paul Shorey as vice-president. The cause of the classics was fortunate in the selection of these two men, who were among the most formidable spokesmen for liberal education in the country.

After the completion of thirteen volumes of *CJ*, an Index was authorized and published in 1919. In that same year, perhaps suitably at a meeting in Atlanta, discussion began about the establishment of a southern section of the Association, since the locus of the Association's membership was in the upper mid-west. A regional southern meeting, it was argued, would enable many more people to attend a classical convention.[11]

In 1920, the Association's membership recorded a severe drop, for the first time in its history, with some 300 fewer members. This led to a tighter budget; for the moment, at least, expansion was at an end. The call to the annual meeting echoed with words different from its predecessors:

> The importance of attendance, both to the individual and to the associations, can hardly be overestimated. It is especially important this

year that we have a numerically strong, enthusiastic rally. The years of the war and, worse yet, this post-war year have been lean years to all humanistic studies. Society's morale needs a renaissance of humanism. It has suffered a severe strain through an overdose of materialism and long-continued struggle with material forces. We all need to get back to the arts of peace, to the elevating and refining studies of mind and spirit. We need to assert once more that if life must be spent, as seems just now necessary, amidst the clatter and uproar of material pursuits, amidst raucous declaration and war of words, amidst strikes and race riots, and demoralizing struggles with the high cost of living, our only hope of salvation to sanity and the ultimate triumph of higher civilization is to keep alive and brightly burning the ancient flame of higher learning. If we must scrub floors, let us scrub them with our hands and not with our souls. Let us rally to our annual meeting and both contribute and receive new inspiration and encouragement for the advancement of the cause of classical studies.[12]

"The cause of classical studies" faced similar pressures in England. At just about the time that the American Classical League was born, Oxford University was considering the place of compulsory Greek; after hot debate, a new Statute was passed which provided that Greek would be only one of a variety of subjects in the preliminary examination (Responsions) for an Honours course. Further discussion of the role of classics followed.[13]

Those who were convinced of the value of Greek studies were more than ever concerned to prove they were worth while and recognized to be so by those who controlled entry into the non-specialist professions. The introduction to part I of the Report was clearly drafted very largely by Murray[14] and is a good statement of the case for classical studies. A knowledge of the Greek and Latin classics, it is argued, gives access to literature which is often thought the noblest in the world and is at the least unique and irreplaceable (translations even of the historical and philosophic works cannot give the full value of the original). Classical literature enables us to study civilizations in which many problems similar to those of our own age appear, but in simpler form and on a smaller scale. And the training for an understanding of the classics exercises many different parts of the mind—memory, imagination, aesthetic appreciation, and scientific method.

The Committee took evidence from a large variety of witnesses, representing professions or giving individual views. Those from the business world were unanimous in regarding premature specialization as a mistake, and the committee were able to argue that the position of classics in education had received serious and sympathetic consideration from many quarters hitherto regarded as hostile.[15]

Classics had been dethroned; how they would be able to respond to new circumstances was the large question at the beginning of the nineteen twenties.

NOTES

1. CJ 11 (1915-16) 193.
2. *ibid* 193-194.
3. The address appeared in CJ 12 (1916-17) 501-521.
4. *ibid* 81.
5. A. F. West, ed., *Value of the Classics* (Princeton 1917). Pp. vii, 396.
6. David Magie (1877-1960) was Professor of Classics at Princeton University from 1911 to 1945. His greatest work, *Roman Rule in Asia Minor* (1950), received the American Philological Association's first Award of Merit in 1951.
7. CJ 13 (1917-18) 81-87.
8. Andrew Fleming West (1853-1943) was Giger Professor of Latin at Princeton University from 1883 to 1928 and Dean of the Graduate School from 1901 to 1928. He is best remembered as an educational statesman and a staunch defender of the "old," classically-based education.
9. CJ 15 (1919-20) 1.
10. *ibid* 2.
11. For this movement, and all else relating to the Southern Section, see G. H. Thompson, *A History of the Southern Section of the Classical Association of the Middle West and South* (Athens, GA 1980).
12. CJ 15 (1919-20) 195.
13. D. Wilson, *Gilbert Murray OM 1866-1957* (Oxford 1987) 258-259.
14. Gilbert Murray was Regius Professor of Greek at Oxford University from 1908 to 1936.
15. Wilson (above, n. 13) 259.

# FOUR *The Decade of the 1920s*

AS THE DECADE OF THE 1920s BEGAN, the Association approved the first major change in its structure since its foundation. The call for a separate southern branch, which had been issued at the Atlanta meeting in 1919, met with approval. The formation of this unit, which was to be known as the Southern Section, was authorized and monies granted to help defray expenses. The first meeting was scheduled for Columbia, SC, in February 1921.

The reader will recall that the Publicity Committee had published a pamphlet entitled "Arguing with Bob" a few years before. It had a wide success, and led to expansion of the program.

## NEW "BOBS"

A new edition—the sixth—of the little pamphlet "Arguing with Bob" issued by the Publicity Committee several years ago, has just been published. More than thirty thousand copies of the pamphlet have been circulated, but it has been out of print for some time. The Committee anticipates a new demand for it as soon as its reissue is known.

A new pamphlet in Latin, entitled "Robertus ad Patrem" has also been published. Professor H. C. Nutting of the University of California is the author. Like the other "Bobs" the new pamphlet is in the nature of a brief dialogue presenting the cause of the classics.

Printing costs are now so high that the Committee has been obliged to increase the price of the pamphlets, though they are still cheap. Following is the scale: "Arguing with Bob," 12 pages, three cents each, 65 cents for twenty-five, $2.50 for one hundred; "Robertus ad Patrem" two cents each, 45 cents for twenty-five, $1.75 for one hundred.[1]

The foundation of the American Classical League came about in order that there might be a national organization, embracing classicists at all levels, to fight against the pressures now facing the study of the ancient languages. Early in its life it undertook a survey which was to prove to be an extremely important public examination of the state of Greek and Latin in this country and a statement of measures which could, and should, be taken in their behalf. Indeed, the most significant event of this decade affecting the classics was the classical investigation. An editorial in *CJ* informed the membership of the new undertaking.

## THE CLASSICAL SURVEY

A classical investigation under the auspices of the American Classical League has been authorized by the General Education Board.

Dean West, president of the League, has given out the following statement:

I am authorized by the Officers of the General Education Board to announce that the General Education Board has appropriated $60,000 to provide for an investigation of classical education in the secondary schools of the United States. The investigation will be conducted by the American Classical League and will probably require three years for its completion. It will be in the general charge of an Advisory Committee, with the co-operation of eight Regional Committees for the following districts: New England, Middle States, the South, Central West, Southwest, Northwest, Rocky Mountain States, Pacific Coast. When the work has been definitely mapped out, three expert investigators will be appointed. The Advisory Committee will ordinarily meet alternately in New York and Chicago. The Regional Committees will meet at such places as may be hereafter arranged. The co-operation of the Regional Committees is a necessary and most important part of the plan. The investigation will have three stages: first, finding the actual facts, so that the existing situation may be clearly known; second, analysis and criticism of these ascertained facts; third, and most important, preparation of a progressive constructive plan for the teaching of classics in the secondary schools of the United States. The timeliness and importance of such an investigation need no comment. At the end of the work a full report will be prepared and published.

The selection of the expert investigators will be announced soon. Advisers in other subjects such as English, Modern Languages and History, may be specially appointed later. The Regional Committees are in process of formation. The Advisory Committee is constituted as follows:

Andrew F. West, Princeton University, Princeton, N.J., Chairman; A. L. Bondurant, University of Mississippi, University, Miss,; W. L. Carr, formerly of University High School, Chicago, Oberlin College, Ohio; Roy Flickinger, Northwestern University, Evanston, Ill.; Mason D. Gray, East High School, Rochester, N.Y.; Richard M. Gummere, Penn Charter School, Philadelphia, Pa.; Gonzalez Lodge, Teachers College, Columbia University, N.Y.; W. V. McDuffee, Central High School, Springfield, Mass.; F. J. Miller, University of Chicago, Chicago, Ill.; Henry Pennypacker, formerly of Boston Latin School, Harvard University, Cambridge, Mass.; Frances E. Sabin, University of Wisconsin, Madison, Wis.; Julius Sachs, New York City; A. T. Walker, University of Kansas, Lawrence, Kan.; W. R. Webb, Jr., Bellbuckle School, Bellbuckle, Tenn.

It is a matter of great congratulation that we are at last to have a thorough investigation of classical education in our American schools, an investigation which will be extensive, deliberate, and impartial. In so doing, we shall seek to ascertain just what are the excellences and the defects of our present methods and what should be done to organize our entire school classical education on an improved basis for the future. In particular, we shall lay special emphasis on the methods and spirit of our teaching. Although, as a matter of fact, we already know that classically trained pupils usually do better than those who are not classically trained, we are also conscious of serious faults in our teaching methods, not so bad, indeed, as in most other subjects, and yet faults which need sharp correction unless classical education is to suffer serious harm. We shall welcome expert information, both from friend and foe, on this and on all other important problems with which we have to deal. We shall expose our own faults and seek to correct them, believing that in this way we shall best convince the public of the genuineness and importance of what we are doing. And, above all, it will be our purpose to place the teaching of the classics on a living, modern, humanistic, and humanizing basis, free from the two extremes of pedantry and superficiality, and thus waken in full power the real influence of the classics as an invigorating, pervading, enlightening force in our education. Let in the light![2]

The year 1920-21 was in several respects a disappointing one in the Association's history. The membership loss of previous years was recovered, reaching an all-time high of 1999 in March 1921, but the Association showed a deficit for the first time, a sum of $602.51. This was largely caused by an increase in the cost of publishing CJ of just above $1837. As a result, the printing contract with the University of Chicago Press was terminated and a new publisher found in Menasha, WI, who offered a much lower price. After the publication of sixteen volumes of *Classical Journal*, the University of Chicago had no formal connection with the Association.

Further measures to remedy the Association's finances were taken. The number of pages of some issues of the *Journal* was reduced to forty-eight; after seemingly constant growth and expansion, retrenchment had begun. An advertising section was introduced, which proved to be both profitable and useful. Circulation was above 4,000, which made it the largest periodical of its kind.[3]

The overriding question of the day, the state of the study of classics, particularly Latin, in the schools, continued to command a great deal of space in the *Journal* and thought everywhere. An extensive editorial in December 1921 speaks boldly.

## THE ELEMENT OF INTEREST

The proper place of interest in the educational scheme is a question much complicated by the extremists who profess to be experts, but whose main business too often seems to be to get glory to themselves by supplying a "scientific justification" for what the public appears to want. It may be well, therefore, to look into this question somewhat dispassionately.

In the first place, however highly we may rate the value of a prescribed course of study, and though we may hope that the pendulum will ultimately swing back in that direction, the fact remains that for the present, and for some time to come, the study of Latin will be mostly on an elective basis.

Second, it is not to be expected that, on a purely elective basis,

Latin will be able to hold its own automatically in the schools. For whether or no the high school student is at an age when he may safely be trusted to select his course of study wisely, as a matter of fact he is pretty much at liberty to choose what he will; and Latin does not enjoy the reputation of being an easy and attractive subject.

Under these circumstances, it is clear that it will no longer serve baldly to offer the old Latin course of the days of prescription, bidding the student take it or leave it; in most cases he will be only too glad to leave it. Rather, some definite plan of campaign must be developed to meet the new conditions.

Of course, considerable progress has already been made under this head; for example, in the direction of the attention of parents to the school work of their children. Literature for use in this connection is now fairly abundant; and both parents and administrative officers are impressed by concrete exhibits designed to show the "practical" value of the study of Latin, notably its relation to the pupil's command of English, a subject to which much attention has been given of late.

If we are left to deal with the student himself, it is his interest that must be appealed to in some way or other; for it does not accord naturally with high school age to forego present ease and pleasure in favor of hard work that may later yield valuable fruit. It is the impulse of youth to seize the desired thing that is within reach, and to take a chance in regard to the future.

Especially in the larger schools, attractive extra-curriculum activities abound. These take time; and if equal credit toward graduation and college matriculation is given for subjects that involve little drudgery, why tie one's self to a "grind," especially in view of the fact that the great lights in education have made the joyous discovery that "the educational value of all subjects is the same"? A practical illustration is seen in the case of a lad who found that he had not the time to keep up with his Vergil class, and transferred to a "science" in which the back work could be read up in a day or two, and full credit secured by taking a little test on the same.

In college work, too, a like difficulty is being encountered. Here the pressure of extra-curriculum activity is at the maximum; and the vastly increased enrolment of late years almost inevitably is establishing as the norm the huge class that runs up into the hundreds, and which meets a lecturer three times a week, laughs at his jokes, reads a book or two, passes a test,—and registers three units toward graduation.

A subject like mathematics, which is still prerequisite in so many lines of work, holds its own pretty well even against such competition; but the case of the classics is hard indeed. Few students have the time and the will to submit themselves without compulsion to the demands of a course that ties them down to regular careful preparation. Partly to meet this condition, and partly to enroll more students, college departments on every side are setting up Greek and Latin courses in English.

Such courses offer the student something that he can handle with as little difficulty as a lecture course in economics, let us say. Meanwhile prophets are not wanting to spread the glad news that everything of value in the study of the classics can be reached through translations, and that while others foolishly fought to win the prize, it is now possible to be carried to the goal on flowery beds of ease. Without pausing to consider this question, it is suggested that college departments of classics will do well, before instituting courses in translation, to consider what effect this action will have upon the genuine study of the languages and literatures concerned. Under present conditions of college work a grave danger lurks here.

Returning to the problem of the schools, aside from spirited and up to date teaching, how may we legitimately appeal to the student's interest? Latin plays and Latin clubs have proved helpful; and, in general, they are to be recommended, if they can be introduced without sacrificing the real business of the course. The inroads that they make upon the student's time need to be carefully watched.

Some recent discussion in the *Observer* touches upon an element of interest which most of us would heartily endorse as in the highest degree desirable. The main proposition follows: "Hard languages are good for boys, as bones are good for puppies' teeth. But the teleology of the bone would be falsified, if the puppy did not find it attractive enough to persevere with." These words inspire an elderly correspondent, who designates himself "Old Crock," to give an account of his own experience with Latin when a lad. He confesses frankly that he was quite at sea at the start, and opines that he never would have succeeded but for the good management of his coach.

The idea of the latter was simplicity itself. He began with the general sense of a passage as a whole, later developing the details and the grammar. As soon as the boy grasped the idea of the passage, and saw that his author really had something to say, he felt that he was getting a return for his effort; in other words, his interest was aroused, and the battle was won.

Unless we belong to the extreme group which holds that in the schools "Latin should not be taught as an end in itself," we shall probably heartily agree that the boy was right in requiring, as a condition of his interested coöperation, that he should be made to feel that, in dealing with a Latin author, he was coming into contact with a real personality and an intelligible message.

It may not be pleasant to face the fact; but it is undoubtedly true that numerous students in the schools have never found their feet in Latin, and flounder about in the manner of the lad above referred to. If anyone doubts the accuracy of this statement, he is referred to the reports rendered from time to time by Professor McCrea on the results of the examinations of the College Entrance Board. Confronted with an easy passage, many a student attacks it without hope of extracting any sense from the Latin, and offers a "translation" consisting of a jumble of English words that mean nothing to him or to the reader.

Under such conditions, how can we expect a pupil to be interested in Latin? And are we not in duty bound to search diligently for ways and means to supply the essential basis of interest that only a real understanding of the text can afford? Under this head two suggestions are offered:

1. Filling the gap between the beginning book and Caesar. At this point of abrupt transition, thousands fall out of step and can never regain their place in the line. Already very promising signs are seen in the growing popularity of the plan whereby beginning Latin is spread over three half-years. On this basis it is possible to lead up to Caesar by means of easy graded readings; and with such preparation, in some schools at least, it is found feasible to read four books of Caesar in the fourth half-year, with noteworthy gain in efficiency and interest all along the line.

2. Reorganization of the work of the third year. So far as the fourth year is concerned, Vergil seems to meet the requirements as well as any author could; but for the third year it is questioned whether six orations of Cicero form an ideal programme. At least three things can be said in its disfavor.

First, though a competent and devoted teacher can handle the orations in such a way as to make the study exceedingly valuable, the content of such a course lacks in attractive power; at any rate our heaviest loss in enrolment is just at that point. With more attractive reading matter in the first half of the third year, more students might be induced to continue the subject beyond the two-year minimum.

Second, in view of the slow progress in the reading (six orations in a whole year), there is too much sameness in the programme. Even in college classes, which cover ground so much more rapidly, the student wearies of the sameness of his text, and it is often found a good plan to include two authors within the limits of a single half-year.

Third, the thought units are too large to be handled comfortably by young pupils who know little Latin, and who perforce must proceed very slowly. Thus it is said that the Manilian Law is easy; but even the earnest student easily gets lost in the largeness of the treatment, and is often quite mystified as to what it's all about. A series of stories, each complete in thirty or forty lines, would serve infinitely better as a starting point.

Cicero's Orations, of course, would be retained for the second half of the third year. But cannot we make a legitimate appeal to the interest of our pupils by providing a more attractive menu for the first half of that year? Specially helpful at this point would be a collection of readings that reveal with come clearness the everyday life of the Romans. Here something could be learned from the methods adopted by modern language teachers.[4]

Membership in the Association and circulation of its *Journal* continued to increase dramatically over the next several years: in the spring of 1922 the figures were, respectively, 2550 and 3996; in the spring of 1923, 2947 and 4528; in the spring of 1924, 3258 and about 4900; in the late summer of 1924, 3875 members, with 5076 copies issued on April 1. The mood of the Association improved markedly, along with the strengthening of finances and resources. The crisis in education now seemed a little less grim. A new problem arose and needed to be met, a surprising one considering the threats to the very existence of classical education in the schools only a few years before, namely the shortage of trained teachers. For the first time an editorial on the subject appeared.

Among the most insidious arguments used by those who would discourage the study of Latin among high school and college students is that this study has been falling off to such an extent in the schools that there is less and less demand for teachers of Latin and soon there will be none at all. The vocational incentive, that of studying in preparation to teach Latin, is thus quenched at the very source.

This statement is a poisonous and wanton perversion of the truth, and must be vigorously combatted by those who know the facts and would not see our supply of Latin teachers to a dangerous degree imperilled.

We have been at some pains to discover the truth as to the demand for Latin teachers in the country and the way in which this demand is being met. The fact revealed by our investigations is that there is an urgent and wide spread call for teachers of Latin and an altogether inadequate supply of well prepared, or even ill prepared teachers to answer this call.

◆　◆　◆　◆　◆　◆

So far, then, from being a matter of discouragement to those who would prepare to teach Latin, the present status is a loud and imperative challenge to many of our best and most ambitious young men and women in both high school and college to devote themselves to a subject to the teaching of which, for centuries past, hundreds of the brightest students in every generation have been drawn.

This demand for Latin teachers might arise because of a decreasing supply of teachers due to the spread of the discouraging propaganda mentioned at the beginning of this editorial, or it might arise because of the decreasing number of students of Latin in the schools. But this latter cause at once disappears before the undoubted fact that the *number of students studying Latin in the secondary schools of the United States has been increasing very rapidly in the last few years*. The statistical summaries now being tabulated by the United States Bureau of Education in Washington prove this conclusively. Our latest advices also show that the enrollment in Latin slightly exceeds the total combined enrollment in all the other foreign languages[5]

The twentieth annual meeting, held in Lexington, KY, featured a roll call of past presidents and secretaries and addresses by two past presidents. W. G. Manly of the University of Missouri, the Association's founding father and first president, invoked "Reminiscences," and Gordon J. Laing of the University of Chicago, the fifteenth president, presented "A History of the Classical Association of the Middle West and South."[6] The occasion was marked by the admission of the first Canadian province, Ontario, to membership.

The year 1924 also saw the completion of the classical investigation and the publication of the first part of its extensive report. Dean West's statement to the meeting of the American Classical League was featured in the first issue of CJ's volume 20. It offered further encouragement at the mid-point of the decade.

The most extensive and searching investigation every made of the classics in our schools, or of any other school study in our land, has now been concluded. It has taken three years and has covered the whole country.

The co-operating forces which have brought about this result are the General Education Board, the seventy members of our classical committees, national and regional, forty-eight professors of education and psychology, the United States Bureau of Education, the College Entrance Examination Board, the Department of Education of the State of New York, all the State Superintendents of Education, the Registrars of practically all our American colleges, the various classical associations, over eight thousand teachers who have given their services without compensation, and also leading educational officers of Great Britain and France. This list gives some indication of the immense amount of work which has been done. Many public meetings have been held, many articles have been published, and the amount of traveling done by members of the classical committees exceeds 160,000 miles. In this way the meaning of the investigation has been brought home directly to all parts of the country.

The small special Investigating Committee which supervised the actual conduct of the investigation consisted of Andrew F. West, Chairman, W. L. Carr, Mason D. Gray, and W. V. McDuffee. When their labors were concluded a General Report was drafted and submitted a month in advance to the national Advisory Committee and the Chairmen of the Regional Committees. After three days of discussion and amendment it was unanimously adopted and is now ready for the printer. It will make a book of about 350 pages and we hope that it will be published and distributed in September. This General Report forms Part I of the results of the investigation. There are five other Parts to follow. Part III is now ready. It contains an account of the classics in England, France, and Germany for the last thirty years, including the period since the World War. The remaining Parts are not yet ready for publication, but we hope to publish all of them within two years.[7]

Only a few leading points can be mentioned here. First of all, the Report is based on full statistical knowledge, newly devised scientific tests, special historical studies, and collections of expert opinion. To eliminate any bias of judgment which might be attributed to the investigation if it were conducted entirely by classical teachers, the collaboration and criticism of forty-eight professors of education and psychology has been secured and has proved of great value. We have sought simply to ascertain the facts, favorable and unfavorable, and to discover their meaning. This has been done thoroughly.

Second, we have sought for the true aims or objectives, the proper content, and the best method of classical teaching in order to discover our faults and improve our teaching. This has been one of the most laborious and fruitful parts of the work. In the same way we have endeavored to improve the organization of the course of study and to devise a progressive plan for the future. We believe we have succeeded in doing so.

Third, it is now made clear by evident proof that the way to secure this most desirable and attainable result is to lay great stress on early acquisition of power to read and understand the classical languages and also concurrently and constantly to emphasize the larger permanent values, historical, literary, disciplinary, and practical, which are derivable from proper training in the classics. We emphasize throughout the humanistic as opposed to the pedantic spirit. We believe this is the way to kindle enthusiasm and to awaken in full power the best energies and highest aspirations of students and teachers alike.

Fourth, we find that the two things which now need most urgent attention are the better organization of the course of study and provision for training classical teachers.

In reorganizing the course we propose to introduce easy Latin reading early and to reduce somewhat the amount required in the classical authors, believing it to be better to read a less amount well than a larger amount poorly. We also lay great stress on practice in sight reading.

But the securing of better trained teachers in much larger numbers is our chief problem. All our researches converge on this point. If we can get the well trained teachers in sufficient abundance, we believe that the rest will take care of itself. We have many such teachers now, but the demand is very far in excess of the supply. If anyone wants to make sure that our classical teaching shall produce its full beneficent effect on a large scale for a long time to come, here is the way to make it sure: Give us now the thousands and thousands of well trained teachers we so imperatively need.

Fifth, notwithstanding our faults and failings, the Latin pupils (and even more the Greek pupils) are on the whole the best students in our schools. This is now a matter of definite proof. They are the pupils who usually do better than the non-classical pupils in English, modern languages, history, mathematics, and the sciences. All the evidence points this way, and so perhaps we need not worry greatly as to what all the reasons are. But one reason is evidently that the classical pupils do not shirk from training and do "stand the gaff" better than others.

Sixth, we find that while the enrolment in Greek is deplorably small, it is increasing. The enrolment in Latin is growing by leaps and bounds *and now slightly exceeds the combined enrolment in all other foreign languages*. Remember that this is in spite of the great diversion of educational energies to "practical" subjects during the war. So far as Latin pupils are concerned, we never have had such a flooding in of them. Can we get the teachers to handle them? That's the question.

Seventh, we find that England, France, and Italy have reorganized their secondary schools since the war and have notably strengthened the position of their classical studies,—France most of all. No reconstruction has yet been effected in Germany.

Eighth, the Report discusses the bearings of our classical schooling on the wider problem of the needed reorganization of our entire secondary education.

Ninth, the tide appears to be turning in the right direction in our schools. Simplification of the course of study, better teaching and emphasis on training in the few essential studies of most general *educational* value, continuity and coherence in the pupil's work,—these are the indicated lines of what we hope is to be the coming reconstruction of our secondary schools. Whenever that happens the colleges will be able to stand more strongly on a sound schooling and will be helped to do better college work.[8]

The second half of the decade was quiet and largely successful, marked by optimism and continued growth. The publication of the Report of the Classical Investigation showed that the study of classics had rebounded sharply from its post-war nadir. For volume twenty-one of the *Journal*, which began in the fall of 1925, an expansion to eighty pages instead of sixty-four for at least several issues was announced. In the event, all issues were on the larger scale, making a total, at last, of 720 pages. In April 1926, with a membership above 4600 and a circulation of more than 6000 for *CJ*, CAMWS could claim to be the "world's largest classical association."[9]

The annual meeting of April 1927 was marked by the presence of a distinguished foreigner. More than a decade had passed since a scholar from abroad had been a feature of the program.

The high-water mark of the program came with the paper of Professor R. S. Conway,[10] of the University of Manchester and president of the British Classical Association. His paper was on "The Chivalry of Vergil," a paper which, we are glad to promise our readers, will appear in a later number of the *Journal*.[11]

Professor Conway prefaced his address by a message of good cheer from the British association to our own, which latter he congratulated on its large membership, its happy alliance with the sister associations of the eastern and far western states, and above all for its remarkable success in securing a circulation of six thousand for its organ the *Classical Journal*, a figure which, he confessed, was almost enough to make the founder and sometime chairman of the Classical Journals Board in England turn green with envy.

Professor Conway brought news also which he thought would be encouraging to all lovers of learning, namely the great increase which had taken place in England since the war in the number of boys and girls studying Latin and Greek. The number of students of Greek has been doubled since 1918, while the number of Latin students has been multiplied by six. This remarkable increase he attributed to two causes. The positive cause was to be found in the efforts of the Classical Association, with its twenty or more branches, which had greatly stimulated popular interest in classical study by making people conscious of the relation of this to the vital interests of everyday human life.

The negative cause (here Professor Conway desired it to be understood that he was expressing only his unofficial and private opinion) lay, he was convinced, in the deliverance of classical study from the grave enmity of a multitude of thoughtful and powerful people. This change had come about by the abolition of the compulsory requirement in Greek which, down to 1919, had been laid by Oxford and Cambridge on all candidates for degrees, in science as well as in literature. The result of removing this requirement, which in Greek (though not in Latin) it was hard to justify, and which in practice had become an exasperating farce, had been, not to destroy Greek, but to double the numbers of those who studied it seriously, that is, for two or three years (not for a mere three months, which had been the time usually given to meet the old requirement), and that, too, in the very schools where the defenders of compulsory Greek had expected it to vanish. Greek was also developing well in the younger universities and the new schools which they influenced.

Whatever the cause, the figures were remarkable and pointed to a real development of public feeling in favor of the classics. In the London *Times* of November 15, 1926, a table appeared showing the expansion in the numbers of the candidates in Greek and Latin under the two chief examining boards, that of Oxford and Cambridge, which had in all subjects about six thousand candidates, and that of the point matriculation board of the allied younger universities, which had more than twice as many. This table showed that, whereas in 1918 there were 805 candidates in Greek and 1794 in Latin, in 1926 there were 1515 candidates in Greek and 11,116 in Latin.

The most encouraging increase was in the schools which looked to the younger universities, the increase in these schools having been more than fivefold in both Greek and Latin. This meant an almost wholly new development in many schools which had never seriously attempted the subjects before. Similar expansion in classical study was taking place in France, and had set in again in Germany after the convulsion of the revolution, and he looked forward with complete confidence to the future of classical studies.[12]

The Association's business and activities were now routine. Only seldom were new initiatives undertaken. In 1927 a committee was appointed to assist in the organization of classical associations, either state or interstate, within the area of CAMWS. This harkened back to the call of Professor Kelsey in 1894 for the establishment of state groups, a desideratum long since not satisfied.

The next year, 1927-28, began with a reaffirmation of the scope and function of the Association's journal and was marked by the presence of another distinguished foreigner at the annual meeting. Volume 23 of *CJ* recalled in its first editorial the very first issue of 1905.

It may be well to state explicitly the ideal which guides the editors in seeking and selecting material for the *Journal*. In brief, that ideal is a volume in which there shall be nothing beneath the consideration of the college professor, nothing which will not benefit the properly trained high-school teacher.

A pair of criticisms will help to explain our position. We quote from memory, but with essential accuracy. A high-school teacher wrote: "Please stop my subscription to the *Journal*. It is written wholly for college professors and does me no good. What teachers want is articles telling us how to teach." An eminent scholar is reported as saying: "What can be done about the *Journal*? It is no good. The high-school teachers have swallowed it up." There is a modicum of truth in both criticisms. The teacher who wants nothing but advice as to methods does find articles which try to give him something to teach, and evidently is sometimes merely irritated by them. The man whose interest is wholly in technical scholarship finds too many suggestions as to methods, too few results of original investigation, too many generalizations of results with which he is already familiar. Taken together, these criticisms delimit the field of the *Journal* as we understand it. There are journals especially adapted to each class.

But we hope that such extremists are few. The *Journal* attempts to carry out the purpose of the Associations whose organ it is, as stated on the last cover-page: "to provide a means of intercommunication between teachers of the classics—whether in the secondary schools, in the colleges, or in the universities of the territory it covers; and generally to promote a unity of thought and action in the broad field of classical teaching." We believe that most teachers of the classics, whatever their field of activity, sympathize with that purpose.[13]

During the course of the year, both membership and circulation dropped slightly, after a purge of those who had become delinquent in their payment of dues. At the meeting in Nashville in April, Joseph Wells [14] was guest of honor. Vice-Chancellor of the University of Oxford and sometime Warden of Wadham College, he spoke on "Herodotus and Athens." At the business session, the Association adopted the following recommendations:

> The Executive Committee reminds the members of the Association of the fact that in the *Classical Journal* for December, 1924, an editorial called attention to the Italian proposal to celebrate in 1930 the twentieth centennial of Vergil's birth. The Committee believes that the time has now come to take definite steps in preparation for the celebration of this event.
>
> It recommends, therefore:
>
> That the Classical Association of the Middle West and South invite all lovers of Vergil to join Italy in thus honoring her greatest poet.
>
> That the editorial staff of the *Classical Journal* be instructed to make the issue of October, 1930, a Vergil number.
>
> That this Association offer a prize of twenty-five dollars for the best tribute to Vergil composed in Latin in a form suitable for a commemorative tablet, reserving the right of withholding the prize if no acceptable tribute is offered.
>
> That the President of the Association appoint a special committee to receive further suggestions and to formulate plans for the proposed Vergil celebration. [15]

The decrease in the number of members continued into the following year, with a net loss of 322 after a purging of 662 persons. Closer attention to renewals of membership had brought greater accuracy to the membership rolls, suggesting that the large figures of recent years had been somewhat inflated. Nonetheless, circulation of *CJ* was little affected, reaching 5870.

The Chicago meeting of late March 1929 was the largest in history, with a registration of 438. Many were obviously attracted by two features of the program, a Round-Table Conference on Elementary Latin chaired by B. L. Ullman and a festive banquet honoring Paul Shorey, which was attended by three hundred people, the maximum permitted by the hall in which it took place. Speakers were Gordon J. Laing of Chicago, Walter Miller of Missouri, John A. Scott of Northwestern, and Shorey himself.

Membership rose substantially during the next year, with parallel growth for *CJ*. It was a quiet year, particularly marked by the sudden death, *aet.* 67, of the Association's founding father and first president, W. G. Manly, on November 28, 1929. He had been Professor of Greek at the University of Missouri since 1890. He surely must have been satisfied with the growth of his institutional offspring. The *Journal* was in its twenty-fifth volume at the time of his death; a large cumulative Index was essential and was approved at the spring meeting. The task was monumental, even taking into account the earlier Index covering the first thirteen volumes and the annual indices. *Classical Journal* had now published 13,196 pages of text!

Some six weeks before Professor Manly's death came the collapse on Wall

Street. There was no mention of this financial debacle in the pages of the *Journal* in the months that followed. But its effects would be devastating in the years to come.

## NOTES

1. *CJ* 16 (1920-21) 66.
2. *ibid* 449-450.
3. *CJ* 17 (1921-22) 119.
4. *ibid* 113-117.
5. *CJ* 19 (1923-24) 193, 195.
6. *ibid* 338.
7. *The Classical Investigation. Part One: General Report* (Princeton 1924, pp. 305) and *Part Three: The Classics in England France and Germany* (Princeton 1925, pp. 203) were the only parts published.
8. *CJ* 20 (1924-25) 1-4.
9. *CJ* 22 (1926-27) 83.
10. Robert Seymour Conway (1864-1933) was Professor of Latin at University College, Cardiff (1893-1903) and Hulme Professor of Latin in the University of Manchester (1903-1929). He was elected a Fellow of the British Academy in 1918. He was co-editor of the first four volumes of the Oxford Classical Text of Livy and author of *The Italic Dialects* (two volumes, 1897), the *Prae-Italic Dialects of Italy*, with J. Whatmough and E. Johnson (1933), and *Harvard Lectures on the Vergilian Age* (1928). It was while in residence at Harvard in 1927 that he attended the CAMWS meeting.
11. The paper was never published in *CJ* .
12. *CJ* 22 (1926-27) 642-643.
13. *CJ* 23 (1927-28) 1-2.
14. Joseph Wells (1855-1929) was co-author of *A Commentary on Herodotus* (1912) with W. W. How and of *A Short History of the Roman Empire to the Death of Marcus Aurelius* (1931) with R. H. Barrow.
15. *CJ* 23 (1927-28) 643.

# FIVE *The Depression Years*

*sperat infestis, metuit secundis
alteram sortem bene praeparatum
pectus:*

AN EDITORIAL IN THE MIDDLE OF THE DECADE OF THE 1930s concluded with these lines from Horace's tenth ode of his second book.[1] No segment of American society was left unaffected by the financial and economic woes which bit deeply into its fabric. Public education, which depended entirely upon tax revenues, and private education, so largely dependent upon tuition charges and investment income, were both severely damaged, with teachers' and professors' salaries frozen or, very often, reduced, the purchase of books for classroom and library reduced or eliminated, and many students withdrawing from school or finding their aspirations for higher education dashed. For subjects as "useless" as the study of the classical languages, survival was extremely difficult and at no point certain. That the Classical Association of the Middle West and South did survive bespoke its inherent strength; that the *Classical Journal* continued to appear testified to the faith and devotion of countless individuals. The officers of this period overcame enormous difficulties and deserved a collective laudation of *bene meriti.*

It had by no means been rare for the actual program of the annual meeting to differ to some degree from that printed only a month before because of illness or other personal reasons. In the early 1930s at least one person could not attend the meeting and take his scheduled place on the program because his bank was closed and his money inaccessible. Nonetheless, the quality of the programs remained high and attendance continued satisfactory.

Only a few years before, the Association's membership and the *Journal's* circulation rose almost constantly. The opposite now occurred, to a shocking degree, as many members found that even the paltry sum of two dollars, the annual membership cost, was beyond their means.

Nonetheless, the entire period was not all gloom. The Association's second quarter century began with the most significant and meaningful issue of *Classical Journal* yet published. The special Vergil number appeared in October 1930. With an additional signature of text and four pages of illustrations, it totalled one hundred pages, the largest number ever. It contained eight articles by scholars from England, Canada, and the United States. On page one, serving as a dedication, was the prize winner in the contest announced two years earlier for "the best tribute to Vergil composed in Latin in a form suitable for a commemorative tablet."[2] The winner was M.H. Griffin of the University of North Carolina.[3]

PUBLIO VERGILIO MARONI
DULCI DECORI TERRAE ITALIAE
MUSIS HOMERICIS POETAE DILECTISSIMO
MEMORIAQUE AETERNA IN ANIMIS HOMINUM
VATI PACIS UNIVERSAE
DIE NATALI BIS MILLESIMO HOC TESTIMONIUM
PIETATISQUE AC CARITATIS
POPULUS AMERICANUS DEDIT DEDICAVITQUE
ID OCT MCMXXX A D

The final issue of the year also received an extra signature, so that the total number of pages for the volume reached 752. Although membership declined by fifty-three, in the figures reported as of the Ides of March 1931, circulation for the *Journal* rose by 216, as there proved to be significant increases in the membership of the sister classical associations. Circulation now stood at 6243.

March also saw the appearance of the *Index to Volumes I-XXV*, which contained some 16,000 entries. And, with one great literary celebration just past, the Association looked forward to another. Approval was given to a proposal to celebrate Horace's bimillenary in 1935-36.

The year 1931-32 was particularly marked by the presidency of the first woman, Lillian Gay Berry of the University of Indiana. Membership decline continued, with a loss of 210 persons, though CJ's circulation rose slightly.

Early in the following year CJ was faced with a managerial crisis. J.O. Lofberg of Oberlin College had been appointed sole editor, ending the practice of a duumvirate which had obtained since the founding of the Association and the *Journal*. But in early November he was compelled to resign because of illness, and soon thereafter, on November 10, 1932, he died. He had been unable to do more than begin labors for the early issues of the new volume. In this emergency, the Association called upon Roy C. Flickinger of the University of Iowa to resume the editorship, which he had held for four years and which he had felt compelled to lay aside after he was elected president of CAMWS and secretary-treasurer of the American Philological Association. Professor Flickinger agreed to resume this third responsibility, thereby becoming a triumvirate all by himself.

The Secretary's report revealed for the first time the dramatic effects of the nation's travail.

The data in the Secretary's report are presented in comparative tables in order that the reader may make his own analysis. Our Association, like all other educational organizations, has felt the effect of the depression. All four classical associations have suffered a loss in membership. The percentages of loss as computed on the total number of subscriptions to the *Classical Journal* are as follows:

Classical Association of the Middle West and South ................... 13.9%
Classical Association of New England ............................................. 4.3%
Classical Association of the Atlantic State ...................................... 7.9%
Classical Association of the Pacific States ...................................... 19.4%

◆ ◆ ◆ ◆ ◆ ◆

In an age when the reading public has become accustomed to editorials written in a pessimistic tone there is little to be gained by setting up a cry of O *tempora, O mores!* When we compare the status of our Association with what has been going on in the business world during the period covered by this report, we have many reasons to be thankful. A large majority of the members of the Classical Association constitute a body of admirers of the classics who will continue to stand steadfastly by the principles to which our Association is committed.[4]

The Association's membership was down 406, circulation of *CJ* 783. And there was a poignant footnote in the Treasurer's Report. A figure was reported as the income from Advertising. "In addition to this amount there was $166 due for the year from responsible firms and $113.74 tied up in closed banks, part of which will certainly be paid in due time." [5]

Professor Flickinger's presidential address, "Our Message in a Time of Depression," was published almost immediately in the May issue. [6] He invited his listeners and subsequent readers to believe that they as classicists had something to contribute in these dark times.

But our present depression is one in morale, morals, spiritual values, and intelligence even more than in financial matters, and certainly in these respects the classics have a message. It is high time that we stood up and said so.

What has become of the spirit which established a prosperous colony in Virginia in spite of the difficulties enumerated at the beginning of my paper? which emboldened the frontiersmen to press through the Indians into Kentucky? which fought with Blackhawk? which enabled the Mormons to push carts containing all their worldly belongings from the Mississippi River to Salt Lake? If these brave men had been like us, America would still be the home of the Red Man. As a recent writer has said: "There is this important difference between the asceticism of the past and that of the present: in the old days, in the name of religion and morality, men were hard on their bodies; today, in the same name, they are relatively easy on their bodies but are hard on their minds."

But where are we to find the pabulum which will restore courage to our hearts, toughness to our moral fiber, and endurance to our flabby muscles? Where better than in the lives of the classical heroes? Leonidas, who counted not his life dear at Thermopylae; Aristides, who valued the title of "The Just" above ephemeral success in the political arena; Socrates, who defied the howling mob bent upon an illegal act and who was condemned to death at his own trial rather than compromise with his opponents; Curius, who sat in his humble hut after celebrating three triumphs and ate turnips contentedly when he was offered a golden bribe by the emissaries of the Samnites and who said that it was better to rule those who had gold than to have the gold itself; Decius Mus, who consecrated his life in order to guarantee the success of his army; Regulus, who gave the Roman Senate wise advice and then returned to die by the hand of Carthaginian torturers; Fabricius, who scorned the offer of King Pyrrhus' physician to poison his master and so rid the Romans of their deadly enemy; the Romans in the mass, who fell in battle formation facing this same Pyrrhus with all their wounds in front, so that he exclaimed that with such troops he could have conquered the world; and those who, in a later generation, dispatched an army from Rome to Spain while Hannibal was encamped before the walls of the Eternal City; or the realtor who bought the very land on which the Carthaginian army had pitched its quarters at only a slight reduction from normal values—such men and countless others shame our cowardice and cringing fears. Plutarch's *Lives* were once the Golden Book upon which the growing youth was fed, and they produced generations of men who braved the Atlantic with frail barks, conquered the dangers of the New World, and crushed down the still greater terrors of the unknown future. It is our duty and our supreme privilege to instill such thoughts into the minds of the young people who are in our care.

◆ ◆ ◆ ◆ ◆ ◆

We need a rebirth of common honesty and of a sense of duty not only in our public servants but in every citizen from the highest to the lowest. Some would derive these qualities from religion, some from philosophy, and still others from the idealism of science. But I maintain that the classics will be found no less fruitful in this respect than any of the others. Some scientists have forgotten Pasteur's words: "A series of judgments revised without ceasing goes to make up the incontestable progress of science. We must believe in this progress, but we must never accord more than a limited amount of confidence to the forms in which it is successively vested." In high school I was taught to explain light in terms of intangible ether, which has now been bowed out of the universe. I was taught an atomic theory which has been revamped so as no longer to be recognizable—and the end is not yet. Without being a fundamentalist one may still believe that the last word is yet to be spoken concerning the theory of Evolution. For two generations successive hosts of scientists inculcated a theory of matter and physical causation with an absoluteness which degraded man in the universe and reduced him to an automation. Now this world has fallen in confusion about them, and judicious scientists realize that the world of sense and feeling is wider than men knew.

However feeble, then, the support which we receive from other sources, we may still be pardoned, after all, for believing with Plato that there is an ideal world beyond and above that of sensuous substance. For the question is really more fundamental than we have hinted so far. If there is a possibility that man has freedom of will, however limited, it at once becomes important what we choose to do with our lives and what decisions we make towards reaching that *summum bonum*. Certainly here the wide, long-drawn-out experience of peoples so gifted and civilized as the Greeks and Romans is of inestimable value and can hardly be matched elsewhere in the world's history for either richness or variety. In their practical life idealism is exhibited not only by the classical worthies already mentioned, but also by Cornelia when she said "These are my jewels," by the Spartan mothers when they enjoined upon their sons "With your shield, or upon it," by L. Junius Brutus who as first consul put his own sons to death when they attempted to restore the Tarquins to kingly power, by countless others scattered through the pages of classical history.

In literature this idealism and high sense of duty are nowhere more convincingly set forth than in Cicero's *De Senectute*, from which I quote these magnificent words (43): *Qui...iudicabant esse profecto aliquid natura pulchrum atque praeclarum, quod sua sponte peteretur, quodque spreta et contempta voluptate optimus quisque sequeretur.* "They judged that there was assuredly something naturally fine and honorable which should be sought for its own sake and which every excellent man should follow while despising and scorning pleasure."

The Abbé Sieyès, when asked, many years later, what he had done during the French Revolution, is said to have replied: "I lived through it." After all, it is something to have done that. Yet I call upon my classical confréres to assume a more significant rôle during the Depression. Public officials may perhaps have no high opinion of our suggestions for financial rehabilitation, for in Hegel's phrase "We learn from history that no one learns anything from history." Nevertheless, more important than our money are our lives and what we do with them and what we get out of them. Here no one has a larger opportunity than the teacher, and you at least agree with me in thinking that the Latin and Greek classics are the supreme vehicle for inspiring the youth of our country to high ideals, honesty in both a private and a public capacity, honorable dealings with all men, and absolute justice to high and low. In this sacred cause I invite and summon you to a holy crusade.[7]

Flickinger's bold clarion call was followed by an editorial in the second number of the new volume of *CJ* which similarly attempted to bring encouragement and reestablish confidence.

## SEPTEMBER IMPETUS

At the risk of seeming didactic we feel impelled to reiterate the exhortation of last year that we realize fully the importance of a good start. And by that we mean as much a good start for the teacher as for the pupil. Your salary has been badly cut and more work has been piled on? That is the case with most of us all over the country. Smile and keep the classroom cheerful. You could not attend the summer session at your university because of shortened funds? Start the practice of reading new Latin and the translation of works in allied fields. Accumulate new and fresh material from the works of commentators and note how much more easily the business of teaching is carried on. Be composed, overlook small annoyances, avoid indiscriminate talking and yet be interesting to your pupils, and be not guilty of that greatest sin, hurrying for the sake of covering the assignment. A healthy state of the Classics in high school and college depends now more than ever upon cheerful, well-informed, hard-working Latin teachers.[8]

This was followed in the next issue by a plea from the secretary, reminding the membership what the Association offers them. Nonetheless, the downward trend continued, with a loss of 284 members as of March 15, 1933, with CJ's circulation reduced by 760.

A charter member called the secretary's office a few days ago and offered profuse apologies for not having sent in her dues and asked: "Is it too late to pay now?" The secretary's reply to this conscientious devotee to our cause was just what yours would have been: "It is never too late."

Have you overlooked payment of your dues for the current year? If so, it is not too late for you as an individual member; but when hundreds of members postpone payment of their dues, as is the case at the present time, the Association finds itself without funds to meet its current expenses. Have our readers observed that the latest volumes of the *Journal* are larger by one-third than those of a decade ago and that the subscription price has not been increased since 1917? Would the members of our Association and the subscribers to the *Journal* wish to have us go back to the smaller numbers, with the size and number of the articles reduced, the "Notes" and the "Hints for Teachers" and the "Book Reviews" cut in half or dropped entirely? An examination of the secretary-treasurer's report in the following pages may suggest that such a reduction of the size and scope of our *Journal* may be necessary unless all members will share in the work of securing new members or new subscriptions. The Association and its *Classical Journal* cannot exist save through membership fees and subscriptions.[9]

On a more cheerful note, plans were maturing for a Horatian Cruise and Pilgrimage for the summer of 1935, sponsored by CAMWS and the American Classical League in cooperation with the Bureau of University Travel. "In richness of experience and in pure enjoyment the *Bimillennium Horatianum* ought to surpass even the *Bimillennium Vergilianum.*"[10]

At the Memphis meeting of 1934, the Association supported a recommendation of the Executive Committee and endorsed the following conclusions and recommendations of Committee Q of the American Association of University Professors, a committee appointed to investigate the problem of required courses in Education:

"The committee believes that it is an opportune time for this Association to express its view on the professional requirements [courses in Education] imposed upon high school teachers. The judgment of the Association as to what the American high school should be and as to the manner in which ideals for it are likely to be attained through teacher training is worthy of the fullest consideration at a time when a national appraisement of secondary teaching is being made.

"The Committee recommends that the Association endorse the following views:

"1. There is no reliable evidence that professional requirements have resulted in an improvement in secondary instruction at all commensurate with the amount of the requirements.

"2. A considerable lowering in the requirements would result in economy and would not lessen the effectiveness of instruction in the high school. There is, in fact, reason to believe that, on the average, teaching would be improved through a possible increased knowledge on the part of the teacher of the subjects he teaches or of related subjects.

"3. A maximum of twelve semester hours is ample to cover that part of professional training which can be regarded as essential for the beginning teacher who has a bachelor's degree from a standard college or university and who qualifies for teaching an academic subject. The training should involve practice teaching and methods, the methods course being closely integrated with the practice teaching. Courses in psychology or educational psychology, when these are required, should be counted toward the requirement.

"4. Some of the general courses which are now taken before a person has taught would be far more significant after he has had two or more years of experience. They should, therefore, not be a part of pre-service training. They should be moved into the graduate school, where they could be given a more substantial character.

"5. The basis for renewal of certificates or for advancement should not stress professional study unduly but should give emphasis to further academic study. Only in unusual cases should the total hours of professional work exceed twenty in the case of a person holding a master's degree.

"6. The basic idea underlying certification of high school principals and other officials, when special certification is required, should be very carefully considered. It should not be forgotten that such persons have a wider and deeper function in education than the mere discharge of administrative matters. Certification requirements should not emphasize one type of qualification to the neglect of others."[11]

Among the other questions which this meeting debated were whether the Association should be involved in the formulation of minimum requirements for the teachers of Latin within the territory of the Association and whether the Association should sponsor a registration bureau for unemployed and properly qualified members, publicity about which would appear in the *Journal*. The former passed, the latter failed of adoption, but the matter was referred to the Executive Committee. It is clear that many Latin jobs were held by individuals without the necessary qualifications, while others, who were well-trained, were without employment. The problem was not an easy one to solve, since many of the former group were specialists in other subjects who had been assigned to teach the bit of Latin that continued to be offered.

By November 1934, the Roosevelt administration had been in office for slightly more than a year and a half. The vigorous innovations of the New Deal were beginning to turn the tide. Difficult days still lay ahead, but there were promising signs as well. The Association's president, Frederick W. Shipley of Washington University, offered encouragement but also somber realism in an editorial:

> Like all other organizations of a similar nature—one might almost say like all organizations—our Association has felt in the last four years the effects of the depression. This was inevitable with secondary school teachers receiving reduced pay, scrip, or no pay at all and with a pretty general cut in budgets and staffs in institutions of higher learning. During the past five years the state vice presidents have done heroic work against great odds in their various states to keep up the membership of the Association, and it is indeed surprising that they have succeeded as well as they have. The loss in membership, while considerable, has not been greater than might have been expected under the circumstances.
>
> From all indications the tide now seems to have definitely turned. The Secretary reports that Latin is beginning to come back in the high schools, schools that have been in arrears in paying their teachers are beginning to pay again, and from all over the country come reports from colleges (as yet unofficial) of substantial increases in enrollment. In my own institution the increase in Latin and Greek has been marked, and this increase is not likely to be an isolated case when we get the returns from other colleges.
>
> Speaking for the Executive Committee as well as for myself, may we not bespeak your coöperation in taking advantage of this turn of the tide, first, by paying your own dues early in the year in order that outstanding bills may be met and, second, by helping to secure additional members? If each member could be responsible for one new member, the membership of the Association would exceed any figure that we have reached in the past. This is no impossible achievement. Talk with your new colleagues who have never been members and with old members who have dropped out because of financial stress, also with friends of the classics in your community who may be interested in our work. Send the names of these prospects to the Secretary of the Association or to the vice president for your state.
>
> Let us make it our first goal to restore the *Journal*, which on account of decrease in revenue has had to be cut to sixty-four pages, to

its former eighty pages. The *Journal* is a most important factor in classical education in this country and a type of journal that since its inception has been imitated in several countries in Europe.

As a second objective, let us, through the momentum of increased numbers, carry out the two important plans proposed in the Memphis meeting last April, namely, to undertake the work of standardizing the requirements acceptable to the Association for teachers of Latin in secondary schools and to endeavor to sponsor a Registration Bureau for unemployed properly qualified members. Both of these projects are highly desirable. The second cannot be undertaken without the additional revenue that an increased membership would bring in.

May we not count upon your enthusiastic coöperation?[12]

The reduction in the size of the *Journal* brought it back to what it had been ten years before. Memberships and revenues had continued to drop; on the Ides of March 1934, there had been a sixteen percent decline, which brought the total of members to 2035, a loss of 391 from the previous year. The *Journal*, with a circulation of 4080, had fallen by 653 subscribers. And the Treasurer's report had shown a deficit, as of August 31, of $290.25, reducing the cash balance to $349.39. The Association had now almost exhausted the cash balances which had been accumulated in the years of prosperity.

The academic year, however, came to an end with the joyful celebration of Horace's bimillennium. The St. Louis meeting featured a festive luncheon.

At this point, halfway through the depressing decade, the Association's fortunes began to improve, along with the general state of the nation. Its financial state turned a corner, with an excess of receipts over expenditures for the year ending August 31, 1935, of $349.06, almost precisely doubling the cash balance. The intellectual highlight of the year was the appearance of the Horace number of *CJ*. The December issue contained a frontispiece of the monument of Horace at Venusia and six papers, all by American scholars.

The annual meeting in Cleveland in April 1936 was one of the most successful of recent years. The invitation to attend which appeared in the *Journal* expressed a renewal of confidence and pride in the Association and its activities. An added attraction for many members was that this meeting was nearer to Canada than at any time since Ontario had been included in the Association's territory more than a decade before.

Nothing is being overlooked that might help to make this the most important and the best meeting of the Classical Association of the Middle West and South in the thirty-two years of its history. Whether it will be so depends very largely on the coöperative help and *the presence* of a large proportion of our membership. We need occasionally to be reminded that this is the most important meeting of classical teachers in the territory served by our organization; that this is the most important professional organization of college and secondary teachers of Latin and Greek in the world; that it publishes the most widely read journal for teachers of classical languages obtainable anywhere in any language;

that we render to our Association only a paltry part of the service due and receive far less than our share of its benefits when we do not attend its annual meetings; that such a gathering of keen-minded people of the same interests from all over the country is something far more than just another teachers' meeting; and that it is due ourselves, our profession, and the best interests of our teaching as individuals to renew our courage, our minds, and our spirits at this fountain of good things and in this mingling of friends of like mind from all parts of the country. Let us, then, begin to lay our plans for going to Cleveland.[13]

On the Thursday evening, after the banquet, which was attended by 260 members and friends, there was a display of oratory which must have pleased the most rhetorically inclined and perhaps wearied others. There were three formal expressions of greetings, one response for the Association, and four addresses, by the Mayor, the President of Western Reserve University, a distinguished newspaperman, and the Association's President, Victor D. Hill of Ohio University.

The Executive Committee received a proposal from the Classical Association of the Atlantic States which, if approved, would have changed the face of classical America dramatically. Under its terms, CAAS would become an allied association of CAMWS, taking its place alongside the New England and Pacific States Associations. The *Classical Weekly* would be amalgamated with *CJ*, which would absorb some of the other's features, and *CJ* would become the sole official organ of CAAS. In other words, *CJ* would be the only publication of all four regional organizations in the United States. This proposal was discussed in the greatest secrecy, not brought to the attention of the membership, and decision postponed until the next year.

In the event, the proposal for amalgamation was expanded to include *Classical Outlook*, the official publication of the American Classical League. The next step was perhaps even more drastic; it envisioned the formation of a Classical Association of America, which would keep both *CJ* and *CW* alive. The Executive Committee voted to keep the tentative action confidential and approved the following by unanimous vote:

> The Executive Committee of The Classical Association of the Middle West and South has been considering for the past two days certain proposals made to our Association by The Classical Association of the Atlantic States. These proposals visualize the amalgamation of all the Classical regional Associations into a national group to be known, perhaps, as The Classical Association of America. The Executive Committee, as requested, has voted to appoint representatives from The Classical Association of the Middle West and South to meet with representatives from the other groups as a Committee which will thoroughly examine the proposals. We hereby give notice that necessary constitutional changes may be introduced at the next Annual Meeting, if found necessary in order to put into effect the proposed amalgamation, if and as approved by the negotiating committee, the Executive

Committee of The Classical Association of the Middle West and South, and the members of this Association.[14]

All readers of this narrative will realize that this proposal was never consummated. The pattern of classical organizations remained the same, along with the multiplicity of publications. The original feeler from CAAS had been made as a response to the difficulties of the depression, but the gloom was gradually lifting. All in all, it was a good year for the defense of classics. The first number of *CJ*'s new volume contained an editorial which proved so popular in the educational community that subsequently the Association authorized its reprinting in 3000 copies and free distribution.

## AN INVITATION TO ALL LOVERS OF LITERATURE

At a time when so much is being said about the value of social studies in the curriculum; when there is clear intimation that literature, especially literature that is couched in a foreign tongue, is of quite doubtful value; it is very desirable that those who believe in the supreme value of works of the spirit, especially of literature, should organize to combat the plebeianism of the modern professional Educator. For this combat the classicists are prepared, for they were the first to be attacked. Modern languages and literatures are now being assailed, and I have no doubt that the same forces will soon turn against English literature as well. In other words, we are called upon to fight against those who think that only that education is worth while which attempts to fit the individual for his immediate physical environment; that music, the fine arts, literature, and even mathematics are as nothing compared with the social sciences.

The study of a language, whether ancient or modern, has as its ultimate aim the enjoyment and profit to be derived from the literature of that language; and in America there can be no other ultimate aim. We used to be told that there was a practical or business objective in the study of Spanish, but the thousands who have studied Spanish without achieving that objective abundantly prove the fallaciousness of such an idea. Europeans unquestionably study a modern foreign language with the confident expectation of speaking it; and they usually do speak it. For the great majority of Americans, however, such practical use can never be; and language study must be justified on other grounds. What are they?

First, for those who do not proceed far enough in language study to appreciate the literature, we agree that "there is just one reason which would justify the study for the 87 per cent who begin it [the study of Latin], but do not continue it beyond the second year—the close connection between the laws of language and the laws of thought, and the peculiar advantages of the study of Latin as an approach to the mastery of the processes of both." What is said of Latin will apply to Greek and almost as well to the modern foreign languages. Clear thought cannot exist without clear language, and the processes of language cannot be clearly understood in an uninflected language such as ours until one has studied at least one other language, preferably an inflected language. This is the ground, it seems to us, upon which all who believe in language study should stand and fight; this is our universal ground, valid even for those who study any language but a few weeks.

But for the few who study foreign languages further we must insist that enjoyment and profit from the literature of a given language are the only objective of great spiritual and practical value. By literature we mean, of course, not only the great works of the creative imagination, but also the scientific and other works which spring from the intellectual activities of a given people at the present time. In other words, those students who become proficient in a language may and do use that language for intellectual as well as spiritual uplift. Moreover, such students, having mastered the processes of thought by mastering the processes of language, will scarcely be guilty of either sloppy speech or sloppy thinking.

In the field of universal thought the modern languages have an additional value as a tool. It is time, for example, that classicists began to insist that college freshmen should know just why a knowledge of French, German, and Italian will prove a prime necessity for all who expect to go far in the field of classics. It is equally important that professors of the various sciences should insist upon the same type of linguistic equipment. Professors in certain fields of history should make clear the value of Spanish. In other words, all freshmen who expect eventually to go beyond the A.B. degree should be well instructed in the necessity of language equipment for higher studies. Even Latin and Greek are tool languages of the highest importance for advanced students in ancient or medieval history.

Accordingly, we classicists give a very hearty invitation to all lovers of language and literature, to join us in fighting to the finish the proponents of a type of education which would give our youth nothing of the past and its spiritual riches, nothing of the present outside of our own country and our own language; would, in short, make of the youth of today both provincials and plebeians, equally unacquainted with both the processes of thought and the processes of language.[15]

Membership was up, the financial state of the Association continued to improve, and the Horatian celebration brought cheer and enthusiasm. A long article by Flickinger detailed the extent of the activities,[16] the most enchanting part of which were the "Pilgrimages."

As I have already indicated, visits to Horatian sites were an important part of the celebration. National Chairman Lord concluded suitable negotiations with the Bureau of University Travel, which is equivalent to saying that the best of arrangements were made and almost faultlessly carried out. Of course the Bureau had other parties which coalesced with ours at various points, but the League regarded as its official group the one which President Carr and I conducted by motor cars from Paris via Geneva, the Mons Cenis Pass, etc., to Florence, by rail to Rome, by motor car along the Appian Way to Bari and Brindisi, and by steamer through the Greek islands to the Black Sea and back to Syracuse and Naples. From Paris to Florence we enjoyed the expert guidance of Professor George H. Allen, of Lafayette University, who conducted us to Caesar's battle fields, visiting many parts of France which are seldom seen by American tourists; at Florence we were joined by Professor Allen P. Ball, of the College of the City of New York; and from Rome to Brindisi we were accompanied by Professor Rollin H. Tanner, of New York University. The cruise on the S.S. *City of London* was under the co-directorship of Professor Lord and Dr. H. H. Powers, assisted by a competent staff which I must not take space to enumerate further. The official party consisted of about thirty-five travelers at Paris and grew by steady accretions to about one-hundred and sixty-five on board ship.

On July 21 some seventy of us, after stopping at Hadrian's Villa and Tibur, engaged in suitable commemorative exercises at Horace's Sabine villa and visited the Horace museum at nearby Licenza. July 26 was the great day at Venosa (ancient Venusia). Here three parties converged. Our group had driven in two days from Rome via Terracina and Capua to Benevento, where we spent the night, and then on to Canosa, Venosa, and Bari. The other two groups came by motors from Bari, one of them having just arrived by rail from Naples and the other having just disembarked from the *City of London*, which had been cruising in the western Mediterranean and the Adriatic. Here also suitable exercises were held, by each of the three parties, before Horace's modern statue in the Piazza d'Orazio. It seems that in the entire history of the town never had more than ten persons visited it in a party. Accordingly one can easily imagine the excitement which arose in an Italian town when first one, and then, after an interval, a second, and finally, still a third motor car, with passengers aggregating over a hundred, arrived on the same day! The little *podestà*, Signor Bartolimo Cancellara, a man of parts with some command of English, was the personification of hospitality. It was here, also, that Professor Carr met his Waterloo. He was accustomed to rally his group by an imitation bugle call, which he had occasion to repeat at Venosa. A small boy witnessed this performance in amazed bewilderment but finally ejaculated "*Il Corriere!*"

All three groups spent the night on board ship at Bari; but the official party, faithful to Serm. I, 5 to the last, continued by motor car next morning and rejoined the others at Brindisi that night, incidentally visiting the famous *trulli* at Alberobello. It is hard to resist the temptation to dwell upon the details, serious and amusing, of all this, especially with reference to the cruise; but I shall succumb to the extent of only one anecdote: In the *City of London* dining room there were twelve assigned to the table over which Professor Carr presided. It was a hilarious group and soon became well acquainted. When we reached Rhodes and began to hear about the Dodecanese islands, someone nicknamed this table "Professor Carr's Dodecanieces!"[17]

The new mood, overcoming despair, was clearly enunciated in the final editorial of volume thirty-two:

The academic year which closes with this issue of the *Journal* has been noteworthy, we believe, for genuine progress in the effort to establish the place of the classics in the much-discussed integrated high-school curriculum.

◆ ◆ ◆ ◆ ◆ ◆

In fact the year has shown that the forces of the classics are better organized than ever before, not to compel an unwilling public to retain in the curriculum a traditional subject of doubtful value, but to convince that public that the classics can and always have, when properly taught, produced men and women who knew how to evaluate the conditions of life around them, to respond properly to those conditions, and to live effectively, thoughtfully, sympathetically, and constructively.[18]

The year also saw the publication of a brief pamphlet, *The Value of the Classics Today*, sponsored by the ACL, the Association, and other groups, which summarized various expressions of support for the classics, from distinguished individuals such as President Nicholas Murray Butler of Columbia University and President Robert M. Hutchins of the University of Chicago.

For the remaining years of the decade, membership and resources continued to grow. In 1939, there were 2273 members, CJ's circulation was up to 4430, the largest figure since 1933, and the Association's available cash had risen to more than three thousand dollars. In 1938, the Association had its first Canadian president, Norman W. DeWitt of the University of Toronto. Earlier that year, one of the most important and active committees submitted its report. It underscored the hot debate which then existed in the world of education on questions of curriculum. Its importance is self-evident, and thus merits full presentation. It laid out a battle-plan for classics at a seemingly fruitful time. Only a little more than a year later war broke out in Europe. The country would turn to matters of more immediate importance than educational curriculum.

## Progress and Problems of the Committee on the Present Status of Classical Education

### By A. PELZER WAGENER
*The College of William and Mary*

It will be remembered that this committee was appointed in 1935 immediately following the St. Louis meeting of the Association. Its purpose was, first, to study the status of Latin teaching in relation to the spreading core-curriculum plan of school organization; secondly, to devise and carry through plans for protecting the study of Latin in the schools, and to promote co-operation between the humanistic fields in combating the extreme tendency toward the domination of education by the social approach. The year 1935-36 was concerned with the first objective. The past two years have been devoted to the second. Some progress has been made, while many problems still lie before us.

The detailed activities of the committee have been presented during the past year in one or two printed reports and in several mimeographed bulletins. Furthermore, "news-letters" have been sent out by certain of the regional directors in our organization. A review at this time may serve, however, as a reminder and as an incentive to effort during the coming year on the part of an increased number of interested Latin teachers.

In general, working organizations have been effected in almost every state in our territory; closer contacts have been established between teachers of Latin; questionnaires have been circulated to arouse the teachers themselves to action, to give a picture of conditions in the various states, and to provide lists of dependable supporters; publicity material has been printed and distributed; conferences within states have been held; new state associations have been formed; classical contests have been revived or started; newspaper publicity has been secured.

Real progress has come in at least one important respect, over which we may really be encouraged. This lies in the fact that there has been an awakening as to the serious situation into which education is being brought, or even has already been brought, by the dominant forces in educational thinking and administration, and by the exaltation of the social studies and of social objectives as the determining factors in the entire educational system. Consequently there has come about the steadily strengthened determination among scholars and teachers in the humanistic fields and among adherents of a sound, reasonable philosophy of education to make a united stand in defense of their principles.

Most significant of what is happening are the thoughts expressed by President Seymour of Yale, as they were quoted in the *Classical Weekly* of March 28. He points out the folly of multiplying courses in the field of the social studies in the belief that better preparation is being given for service to the public welfare. He calls for the salvation and re-invigoration of the older departments and advises that, whatever the future career of the student may be, he "should be placed in an atmosphere where he can draw power from the liberal arts and sciences."

President Seymour is voicing a growing concern and a spreading conviction. Along the same line is a resolution of the Humanist Society of the University of Iowa, endorsing "the movement to combat the present trend toward making the Social Sciences the core of the school curriculum and the resultant elimination of language study and other humanistic subjects." Dorothy Thompson recently expressed similar thoughts in a syndicated newspaper article. The opinions secured by Miss Guyles and Mr. Winspear from members of the faculty of the University of Wisconsin, by a special committee of the Virginia Classical Association from a representative group of Virginians prominent in various fields of occupation, and by Mr. J. W. D. Skiles, of Louisville, from a similar group of Kentuckians show how widespread and how deeply grounded are convictions favorable to our viewpoint, if only they can be made effectively vocal.

The principal undertaking of the Inter-Association Policies Committee, which was formed December, 1936, was to secure financial support from some foundation. While no grant has yet been secured, the attitudes of certain groups which have been approached indicate their realization of the importance of our undertaking and their interest in helping to solve the present problem in the best interest of American education.

One of the first steps taken by our committee was to form contacts with organized groups in other humanistic fields, among them the Modern Language Association and the National Federation of Modern Language Teachers. At the meeting of the Modern Language Association in December, 1936, the president, Professor Carleton Brown, of New York University, delivered his presidential address on "The Assault on the Castle." The result was the appointment of a committee of the Modern Language Association with Professor Howard M. Jones, of Harvard University, as chairman. The committee presented a masterly and voluminous report of forty-five pages at the 1937 meeting of the Modern Language Association last December. The first half of the report deals with the philosophy of modern Progressive Education and its implications in theory and practice for the status of the older humanistic subjects. It puts in logical and impressive form material which our own committee, concerned with the practical problem of trying to combat an existing situation in one particular field, assumed—perhaps erroneously—to be familiar to everyone with whom it would work. The second half of the report is concerned with the activities of the National Council of Teachers of English and presents the results of so-called "progressive thinking" in the field of English upon objectives and methods in that field.

This report has had as a secondary effect the appointment of a special committee by the National Federation of Modern Language Teachers to take steps for the defense of modern language teaching and to co-operate with similar groups in other subject fields.

At the annual meeting of the American Council of Learned Societies in January, 1937 the delegates of the American Philological Association, the Modern Language Association, and the Linguistic

Society of America, pursuant to instructions from their societies, requested the Council to take cognizance of the situation facing the humanistic studies and to confer with other national councils which might also be interested in the matter. Some informal conferences were held. In December last the Modern Language Association referred Professor Jones's report to the Council with the request that the study be continued by the Council on a broader basis by means of a special committee appointed for that purpose.

The meeting of the Council on the afternoon of January 28, at which a discussion of "Recent Educational Trends and the Study of the Humanities" was the special order of business, was most heartening and inspiring. After set speeches by Professor Jones, Dean Henry Grattan Doyle, of George Washington University, and Professor A. P. Wagener, the general discussion was participated in by a large number of those present. It was the unanimous opinion that the seriousness of the situation demanded unified and thorough study of the function of the humanities in education and, upon the basis of the results of this study, unified and vigorous action to insure to the humanistic studies their rightful place. As a result of the resolution passed by the Council, tentative plans for the contemplated study have been formulated. After reviewing the restricted scope of previous similar studies, the report upon the present plan states:

> Its point of view would be that of the humanistic studies as a group. While not attempting to formulate educational theories and philosophies, or to involve new educational practices, it would of necessity concern itself with educational theory and practice, if for no other reason than to remove the maladjustments and misunderstandings that have come into existence between education, on the one hand, and the humanities and most other disciplines on the other. It would also have to take into account the entire educational process, from elementary schools into the vast range of adult education; for a too exclusive concern of humanistic scholarship with the graduate school and research has tended to isolate it on the one side from the sources from which it must seek renewal, and on the other side, from the great body of its ultimate consumers.

The objectives of the study may be briefly summarized as follows:

A. To arrive at some clear conception, if possible, of present educational trends and of the conditions that determine them.

B. To define the humanities in both general and specific terms, and to make clear their community of interest and their relations to other subjects or studies.

C. To ascertain and appraise the educational values of the humanities with especial reference to the life of the individual and the needs of society.

D. To furnish guidance for the fullest possible realization of these values.

At the end of this study, which is assured in some form, a platform will have been established upon which the humanistic subjects may base their claim to a place in American education, and defensible objectives will have been set up. With these in mind each subject may then build its own procedures. The action taken by the United Chapters of the Phi Beta Kappa Society last December in appointing a committee to review standards of recommendation for chapters and membership, and to urge various associations throughout the country "to do what they can toward the re-establishment of the liberal arts emphasis in the schools in their vicinities" is an interesting contribution to these aims. Already the co-operation of many national associations has been promised. We may feel that we are well on the road to a successful culmination of our efforts in one of the most essential undertakings related to the work of our committee.

In the address to which reference has been made, President Seymour says in the very midst of the remarks that have been quoted:

Partly because of their [i.e., the older departments'] trust in tradition and confidence invoked by their former supremacy, they have failed to adapt themselves to the younger generations. The time has come for them to face the necessity of such adaptation. They can save themselves only by answering the demands of intellectual interest.

One of our serious problems is to determine just what such an answer will be. On this there is apparently no unanimity of opinion among classical scholars and teachers. A recent review of the revised edition of an older first-year Latin text condemns its application of the functional approach, its use of "made" Latin, its attempt to vitalize the children's understanding of Roman civilization through illustrations and descriptive material in English, and its omission of the subjunctive mood in conformity with the recommendations of the Classical Investigation. Yet many of us feel the absolute necessity of using many of these approaches, the need of adapting material and procedures to the product of the elementary schools passed on to the teacher of Latin, and the folly of producing texts beyond the range of preparation, abilities, and interests of the children for whom they are intended. One student of curriculum construction points out the value of capitalizing upon the social values of our study, while we find elsewhere a call for the renunciation of the "futile position that the study of Latin has a social value in that it enables children to read stories in 'made Latin' of Roman family life and so on." When, in a certain state, curriculum workers are struggling to develop material, activities, and procedures which will insure the preservation of the sound values of Latin study and yet meet the objectives of general education, common sense would dictate that an article should not be written for the state educational journal condemning these very methods. Yet this has happened. Not that there is lacking sound reasoning in much of the criticism; but it is frequently based on limited understanding of what is advocated and of conditions that must be faced. It is certainly false logic that would lend comfort to the enemy by emphasizing disagreements on technical details. Rather we should attempt to define what are sound, defensible, and attainable objectives in classical study at every level of instruction and be prepared to abide by and to defend our decision. A writer in a recent issue of *Michigan School of Education Bulletin* is right when he says:

> The teachers of children and youth are aware of many chronic ills. It is these that the innovator must expose. And the conservative must consult them also, or forego his right to protest. It is folly for him to cry out from the "parapet"; let him descend and search the foundation for himself. Let him study the children and the school, and then add his voice to the formulation of hypotheses.

The solution of the serious problem of the place to be sought for Latin in the modern high-school curriculum will be hastened by developing a sound and reasonable attitude on the part of our classical leaders which all can accept. To this the committee hopes to contribute through studies and recommendations by its Subcommittee on Curriculum Study, whose findings should be of immediate value for the general study of the humanities. Such a sound and reasonable attitude is vitally necessary at once to our own people, who are confronted by curriculum revisions which are not waiting on us. In Ohio, they are faced by changes to be made in requirements for the preparation of the elementary teachers, which would mean the elimination of foreign language, mathematics, and even natural science, as conventionally organized, from the prospective teachers'-college course. In North Dakota the curriculum is even now being revised and the question is being raised as to the entire elimination of foreign language from the smaller high schools. Curriculum revisions are in progress in West Virginia, Texas, Michigan, Missouri, and elsewhere. The leaders in the fight need to be furnished with sound principles to work for, demonstrable arguments to present, and concrete materials to work with. The establishment of a source of supply to which they can turn is one of our great problems.

We need to assume a diplomatic and sympathetic attitude toward the many educationists and educational administrators who are thoughtful and fair in their attitude and who are earnestly seeking to promote the welfare of American education and of the children of our country. That this is a wise attitude was brought out in many of the speeches made in the discussion before the American Council of Learned Societies. It is foolish to attack all education because of the attitude of an extreme, biased, bigoted, and unscholarly minority even though this group is apparently dominant at the present time, certainly vocally so. We need also to be fair in our claims for recognition and to recognize that there is a proper function for all of the disciplines—humanistic, scientific, and social. We need to develop within our own body a sympathetic understanding and attitude toward the problems and purposes with which those in the various spheres of high-school, college, and university education are faced. Above all, the college and university instructor needs to reach down to the high-school and help the teacher there, with whom ultimately rests the well-being of our subject. He must give inspiration, advice, and practical assistance freely and gladly.

The improvement of teaching is most essential, in fact of paramount importance. Thought should be given by college and university departments of classics to the more functional organization of their teacher-training courses and of their schedules of work for majoring or concentration. These courses should be of such a nature as to provide the prospective teacher with the equipment in knowledge and skills which will make his work with the pupils so successful as to build up an army of advocates for classical study.

The final problem to which attention should be called is one upon which there has been much division of opinion. It is the need for continued and increased favorable publicity, and for the constant cultivation of favorable public relations. In this everyone can help in some of the varied ways that will come to the mind of anyone who thinks about it at all. Spectacular and country-wide undertakings call for expenditures of money which we do not at present have. Possibly funds will come in at some time or other. In the meantime the central committee will supply what it can, and will rely upon the state committees and individual teachers and leaders to contribute their share. Classical people as a group object to both the idea and the term "propaganda." This is not propaganda and let us from now on discard the term. It is presenting to children and to parents of children who should study Latin and Greek the values in those studies they should know of. It is presenting to the public at large the services of our subject in research and discovery, in adding to the intellectual equipment of our people, and in enriching their lives with enduring cultural values. Surely that is dignified, legitimate, and necessary publicity.

Finally, the support of every member of our association is needed through continued labor for our cause, through an attitude of persistent hopefulness, and certainly through gifts to the fund upon which we must rely for carrying on the projects that have been launched![9]

## NOTES

1. *CJ* 30 (1934-35) 514.
2. *CJ* 23 (1927-28) 643.
3. *CJ* 26 (1930-31) 1.
4. *CJ* 28 (1932-33) 163-164.
5. *ibid* 166.
6. *ibid* 561-573.
7. *ibid* 567-568, 571-573.
8. *CJ* 29 (1933-34) 81.
9. *ibid* 161.
10. *ibid* 322.
11. *ibid* 564-565.
12. *CJ* 30 (1934-35) 65-66.
13. *CJ* 31 (1935-36) 274-275.
14. Minutes of the Executive Committee, March 26, 1937, 8-9.
15. *CJ* 32 (1936-37) 1-3.
16. "Horace's First Bimillennium," *ibid* 65-91.
17. *ibid* 81-82.
18. *ibid* 514, 516.
19. *CJ* 34 (1938-39) 1-8.

# s i x *The Second World War*

DURING THE PERIOD OF THE SECOND WORLD WAR, at first survival and then total victory on a world-wide scene occupied most of the nation's attention. All aspects of society were at the service of the war effort. Education was no exception; the need was for individuals who could command science and industrial skills. Save for "necessary" languages and the useful aspects of history and politics, humanistic studies suffered devaluation. This period of extreme national danger proved more difficult for the classics and the Association than even the years of depression had been. Membership was drastically affected by the loss of so many teachers to the armed services, the subject by loss of public esteem. Survival was a constant challenge.

At the beginning of the decade, membership in the Association had fallen to just above 2000, circulation of *CJ* to just above 4200. The last year before the events of Pearl Harbor saw these figures almost unchanged and a continued increase in the cash balance. The Association entered into a financial arrangement with the Classical Association of the Atlantic States to give "attractive combination rates" of subscription to those in the latter organization. These combination rates were subsequently extended to include the American Classical League, so that all classicists in the country who belonged to any of the regional associations or ACL could obtain any or all three of their publications, *CJ, CW,* and *CO.* During 1940-41, the Association had its second female president, Gertrude Smith of the University of Chicago.

At the 1942 meeting, the Secretary-Treasurer, Fred S. Dunham, who was completing a decade in office, took the opportunity to offer not only an annual report but a conspectus of the ten years of his service, which spanned the depths of depression, recovery, and the first year of actual war. In this period the Association had lost 495 members, a decrease of 20.4%. Eight states had lost more than thirty per cent of their membership: Virginia, Kansas, Mississippi, Alabama, Indiana, South Dakota, North Carolina, and Florida.

> Since these states form no geographical pattern, we conclude that the losses must be due to social, economic and educational conditions prevailing in those states, combined with the general trend toward vocational and folk education. It has been a decade of economic depression and violent social movements accompanied by changes in state requirements for the teacher's certificate, an increase in the activities of national and privately supported educational agencies in the general direction of industrial and agricultural training in secondary education, and the development of applied science in higher education. Not only do young people have their sense of values upset, but they frequently find the door of opportunity closed when they wish to continue their studies in advanced classes. They are then told that the limited budget does not permit the

organization of small classes. But these conditions are known to all of us. We are surprised that the Classics have held up as well as they have.[1]

The circulation of *Classical Journal* had fallen from 4733 in March 1933 to 3986 on March 1, 1942, a decrease of 15.7%.

During this year there was an excess of expenditures over receipts because of the activity of the Committee on the Present Status of Classical Education. Continuing efforts in many educational circles to eliminate the teaching of foreign languages in the high schools led the Association to sponsor a response. Written by B. L. Ullman[2] and F. S. Dunham, with the collaboration of John F. Gummere for CAAS and George A. Land for CANE, the article, "The High School's Obligation to Democracy," appeared in the April 1942 issue of *Education*. It was then reprinted as a sixteen page pamphlet, 6000 copies of which were widely distributed over the entire educational spectrum. But the battle was by no means stayed, much less won. The struggle to keep the barbarians outside the gates of the nation's educational system continued without cease.

The December 1942 number of *CJ* inaugurated a new feature with a message from President Dunham.

TO THE READERS OF THE JOURNAL: With this edition of the Journal a new occasional department is born, and Mr. White, who will be its editor, has requested me to officiate at the christening. The innovation will make the *News Letter*, whose circulation heretofore has been limited mainly to members of the Committee on the Present Status of Classical Education, available to all readers of the Journal. Unfortunately we must conserve space. Hence, as Mr. White explains, "It will not be quite so informal and even jocose as it appeared in the *News Letter*," but even so we believe it will be good for our morale, especially during these critical times.

The impact of the war necessarily places emphasis upon immediate efforts to win the war, while plans and preparation for post-war readjustments are held in abeyance. It is true that there is one big job before us, but that task will not cease the day when the last gun is fired. The boys and girls whom we are teaching today will be needed then to guarantee the peace, just as their seniors are needed today in the fighting forces. Even in times of war we must educate for life as well as for death. What doth it profit a man to win the war and lose the peace? Let us beware of the enemy within our gates, whether he be the enemy spy or the misguided "educator" who advocates the elimination from the curriculum of all subjects not directly connected with the war effort.

Preparation for permanent peace is the ultimate goal of the teacher, unless his services are needed in the armed forces. Who is more able than the teacher of the classics to inculcate in our youth the ideals of goodness, truth, and beauty, of law and order, of permanence and tolerance? These qualities, which characterize the democracies, constitute the precious heritage for which we are fighting.[3]

Soon the *Journal* published a letter from a non-classicist, Bayard Quincy Morgan of Stanford University, which states the threat to liberal education in the widest terms. It became, *ut ita dicam*, a battle-cry for the embattled legions.

STANFORD UNIVERSITY, CALIF., JAN. 1, 1943.

AN OPEN LETTER TO TEACHERS OF LANGUAGE.
DEAR COLLEAGUES:

It can no longer be doubted that the American public school is preparing under the guidance of our professional educationists and with the willing or enforced consent of large groups of other educators, to abandon the discipline of formal language study as a foundation stone in American education. No clearer proof of this assertion need be desired than the report of a committee of the National Education Association, presented in June 1942, and entitled "Problems in the Field of Teacher Preparation and Certification." Under the heading "Opinions on the General Education of Teachers," W. E. Peik summarizes the results of an inquiry sent out to 154 persons and responded to by 92 of them, embracing educational leaders distributed over all the states in the Union. As to the inclusion of a knowledge of foreign languages in the general education of teachers, only 14 per cent of the replies approved of modern foreign language for the elementary teacher, only 40 per cent for the secondary teacher; for the classical languages, the percentages were still lower, 13 per cent and 26 per cent respectively. It may therefore be assumed that the rejection of foreign-language study as part of a liberal education is now the official attitude of the National Education Association, which stands for the educationist policy of our country.

It must be recognized, I think, that back of this specific expression of policy lies an educational philosophy which commands a widespread popular appeal. Briefly stated, and somewhat oversimplified, it runs like this: in a true democracy all citizens enjoy the same advantages, and therefore the educational system must be so planned in its intellectual content that every child can share in each part of it, from the lowest stage to the highest. It is the communistic economic argument applied to the realm of the mind. Carried to its logical extreme, such a program would eventually turn the United States into a slave nation, bereft of any leadership which might successfully cope with its brainy and highly trained competitors in the markets or on the battlefields of the world. For if we do not provide suitable training for our future leaders, we shall have none.

Moreover, to one who views the international scene with any concern for the future it must seem that no more inopportune time could have been chosen for thus deliberately reducing the areas of direct contact between the United States and the outside, or non-English-speaking world. All signs point to the inescapable fact that our traditional isolationism is no longer possible or desirable, and that in any event we stand at the beginning of an era of vastly increased American participation in world affairs.

As teachers of language we must necessarily dissent from the conception of American education embodied in the report which was cited above, and in defending our subject against attempts at its extermination we are upholding the prestige and honor of the American school, the dignity and future worth of the American people.

Seeing these precious strongholds of our national heritage thus gravely menaced, what should be our response? Can we afford to ignore the uncompromising attempts to legislate our work out of existence? It seems to me that if we wish to defend its now seriously threatened position in American education, we must have recourse to the strength which comes from united effort, in other words, to voting power, both direct and indirect. Our own aggregate votes constitute a more powerful single unit than any other in the school; the parental vote which we can enlist, if properly directed, is capable of sweeping the country.

The first step, clearly, is for us to get together. As a means to that desirable end, I propose that the various language associations, including those for the Classical Languages and English, send duly authorized delegates to a special meeting in connection with the coming convention of the Modern Language Association. These delegates should be instructed to assist in the formation of a militant association which will have as its principal objective the immediate organization of a campaign to maintain and eventually increase the place of language instruction in the American public school.

It will be the function of the officers of such an association to determine the details of organization and action within which it shall operate. Without presuming to forestall any of their decisions, I suggest that the language teachers of specified areas (e.g. cities, collegiate institutions, districts) automatically constitute "chapters" in the new association, that the chapters of each state form a "division" with elective officers and provisions for convening, and that the real directive of the association be assigned to a national board, subdivided into such committees as may appear desirable, dealing, for example, with policy, finance, and propaganda. As to the possibilities of effective action, I am clear in my own mind that our only hope of substantial accomplishment lies in influencing parents to put pressure on the schools. This requires a long and involved process of public education, and will inevitably call for considerable expenditure. However, if our profession can be sufficiently interested, I believe that a modest membership fee will provide a generous aggregate to serve as the sinews of war.

This letter has no authority beyond that of one who sees an emergency and feels impelled to appropriate action[4]

Further attention to this subject came at the annual meeting of 1943. For the first time, there was a general theme: *Liberal culture in war time - its contribution to the war program and the future peace.* And the final number of CJ's volume offered a very long editorial entitled "Pass the Ammunition." [5]

In the February issue we published an open letter in which Professor Bayard Quincy Morgan, of Stanford University, set forth the necessity for all teachers and friends of language study to combine their strength for the purpose of combating an effort on the part of important and powerful educational groups to "abandon the discipline of formal language study as a foundation stone in American education." If you think Professor Morgan is unduly concerned, read the following declaration of principles recently given great publicity in the "High School Victory Corps Pamphlet No. 1," published by the office of the Commissioner of Education for the United States, and ponder the statements carefully:

A campaign of community education to break down the existing prejudices in favor of the strictly academic college preparatory course is also required. Naturally such a campaign will require the vigorous leadership of the professional educators.

Add to this a statement from the pamphlet entitled "What the Schools Should Teach in War Time," a statement coming from the powerful Educational Policies Commission of the National Education Association:

We recognize the contribution of the ancient languages and literatures to our culture. We believe, however, that a relatively small percentage in any population will achieve from their experience in high school that mastery of these languages which will substantially enrich their culture life. We, therefore, recommend that the teaching of these languages be limited to the very few who will achieve these values and use these languages in their scholarly pursuits.

> The adoption of such a policy would release the time of many competent teachers for educational services vital to the war effort.

To make the position of this group even more clear, its permanent secretary, Mr. W. G. Carr, said in a speech delivered in Detroit, October 2, 1942, and published in the *Michigan Education Journal* for November, 1942, that, since no person in the United States or elsewhere needs to be able to read or write or speak Latin, "either to help win the war or safeguard the peace, I believe that the teaching of Latin as a language should be discontinued at once for the duration, as a high-school subject, required or elective."

There you have it. In the formal printed pamphlet we have hypocritical lip-service: "We recognize the contribution of the ancient languages and literatures to our culture." But when the permanent secretary of this same body tells what he conceives to be the truth, Latin is practically useless "either to help win the war or safeguard the peace."

Let us not deceive ourselves. These are the same educational leaders who have opposed all cultural subjects in the high-school curriculum for more than a quarter of a century. Throughout all that time they have broadened and democratized high-school education, as they are fond of putting it, by lowering standards to the point where almost no one shall fail—as though life were like that. They have denied the superior student his opportunity in order not to give offense to the less gifted. They have persistently substituted training in particular techniques for those hard subjects that develop the capacity to think. Worst of all, they have run off after every new educational nostrum and have by so doing shown themselves unworthy of a following.

Now comes the war. We need good mathematicians, but the high-school graduate fails to measure up to our needs even at the level he is supposed to have attained. We need men and women who can think straight and hard and then express that thought in effective English, and again we find the high-school product unsatisfactory. It is by these fruits that we should judge the "educational leaders" who are now asking the "professional educators" to give vigorous help in the "campaign of community education to break down the existing prejudices in favor of the strictly academic college preparatory course." This "strictly academic college preparatory course," mark you, comprises mathematics, history, English, Latin, French, German, physics, chemistry, and biology. These are the subjects good students take in high school in order to prepare for college, and every one of them is of prime importance both in winning the war and safeguarding the peace. In fact, Colonel Venable of Virginia, who addressed a meeting of college presidents last January in Baltimore to formulate plans for the war, actually declared that he considered the study of Latin the ideal discipline for the soldier. He expressed the view that it teaches the student to think coherently, interrelatedly, and with precision.

But the attack of the "professional educators" has been met by some excellent counter-attack, and it is for the purpose of bringing this helpful material, in part, to the attention of all teachers of the classics and friends of culture that this editorial is written. As Professor Morgan has said, we must get together and fight these cheapening tendencies in our local schools, working through parent-teacher associations, clubs, and especially our newspapers.

We have already called attention to the excellent article of Professor Ullman in the *Classical Outlook* for March, 1943. In the *American Scholar*, current spring issue, will be found the full text of the address of Mr. Wendell Willkie, entitled "Freedom and the Liberal Arts," delivered at Duke University, January 14 of this year. This is the best statement of the case for the humanities we have seen; and it is all the more valuable because it represents the credo of a layman very highly esteemed in public life. Here are some of his paragraphs that will hearten the struggling teacher of the classics:

> For we cannot win a true victory unless there exists in this country a large body of liberally educated citizens. This is a war for freedom—freedom here and freedom elsewhere. But if we are going to risk our lives for freedom, we must at the same time do all we can to preserve the deep springs from which it flows. Recently we have been prone to think of freedom in purely economic terms. It is true that a man cannot be free unless he has a job and a decent income. But this job and this income are not the sources of his freedom. They only implement it. Freedom is of the mind. Freedom is in that library of yours, around which this campus is built. When you range back and forth through the centuries, when you weigh the utterance of some great thinker or absorb the meaning of some great composition, in painting or music or poetry; when you live these things within yourself and measure yourself against them—only then do you become an initiate in the world of the free. It is in the liberal arts that you acquire the ability to make a truly free and individual choice.

Mr. Willkie proceeds:

> President Hopkins of Dartmouth has stated these trends more clearly than anyone I know and has pointed out that

"it would be a tragic paradox if, as a result of the war, we were to allow our system of higher education to be transformed into the type of education which has made it so easy for a crowd of governmental gangsters like Hitler's outfit to commandeer a whole population."

The destruction of the tradition of the liberal arts, at this crisis in our history, when freedom is more than ever at stake, would mean just that. It would be a crime, comparable, in my opinion, with the burning of the books by the Nazis. And it would have approximately the same results. Burn your books—or, what amounts to the same thing, neglect your books—and you will lose freedom, as surely as if you were to invite Hitler and his henchmen to rule over you.

The preservation of our system of liberal education during the war will make an enormous difference in the moral and human tone of our society in the future, of the very atmosphere in which the peace is made, and, since we are not an isolated society, of all civilization after the war. Let me remind you of Irwin Edman's recent fine statement of the significance of the very word "humanities." "It is not trivial art or playful thought. It is the name for the whole of the tradition of civilized life which from the Greeks down has accented freedom in political life and individuality and creativeness in personal relations, creativeness in art, and originality in the experiment of living which is each individual's opportunity. If the humanities, or the humanistic temper which they promote, are permitted to lapse now, we shall have lost the peace before we have gained it, and the real victory after the war will be to the way of life, inhuman, tyrannical, mechanical, of those whom we shall outwardly have conquered."

In pleading for the humanities I am not preaching any gospel of high-browism. The relationship between a liberal education and freedom is good sound American doctrine.

Finally, he says:

We must establish beyond any doubt the equality of men. And we shall find this equality, not in the different talents which we severally possess, nor in the different incomes which we severally earn, *but in the great franchise of the mind*, the universal franchise, which is bounded neither by color, nor by creed, nor by social status. Open the books if you wish to be free. [6]

Invited by Norman J. DeWitt, the Association's Secretary-Treasurer, to express his views on the study of Latin and Greek, the Republican candidate for the presidency of the United States in 1940 replied as follows:

MY DEAR MR. DeWITT:

Thank you very much for your letter of March 3rd. I am indeed happy to have an opportunity to say something about the classics through the medium of the *Classical Journal*.

As a college student, the languages which I studied were Latin and Greek. I have always been happy that it was thus. Indeed I know of no studies which develop precise and logical thinking as surely as does the pursuit of these two languages. I have said many times that if I had to choose between Greek and Latin and some of the so-called practical commercial courses for business training, I would choose Latin and Greek. This, of course, is entirely beside the joys to be found in their cultural values.

Cordially yours,

(Signed) WENDELL L. WILLKIE [7]

The Association continued, over the next two years, its struggle for survival and influence. Membership rose modestly in 1944 for the first increase since 1939, followed by an increase of more than twelve per cent the next year: in March 1945, two months before the European war would end, the total of members was once again above 2000 (2129) and the circulation of CJ almost 4000 (3981). More money continued to flow out than came in, so that the financial resources of the Association required close scrutiny. The Committee on the Present Status of Classical Education was reconstituted as the Sub-Committee on Educational Policy.

The meeting scheduled for Cincinnati in March 1945 was cancelled at the urgent request of the Committee on Conventions of the Office of Defense Transportation. The Executive Committee therefore met in St. Louis at the end of March. The *Journal*'s editor, Eugene Tavenner, retired after ten years of service; in his final editorial he wrote, "During much of our term of office the war has brought very prominently to the fore the question of the proper balance between the *artes humaniores* and the more immediately useful skills, and in this nation-wide discussion of the place of the humanities in our educational scheme the *Classical Journal* has had, and will doubtless continue to have, a worthy place."[8] But in the general gloom the Executive Committee was offered a burst of light, the beneficent consequences of which continue to the present day. Professor William T. Semple of the University of Cincinnati offered to endow an annual fellowship for teachers of Latin within the territory of the Association to attend the summer school of the American Academy in Rome. It would be the Association's responsibility to raise an equal amount in matching funds.

The optimistic view of the place and role of the classics shone forth in this initiative. When the Academy's program would be able to resume, no one could know, but one could be confident that it would do so.

## NOTES

1. Secretary's Report, March 1, 1942, 3.
2. Ullman was Professor at the University of Chicago, he had an extraordinary interest in secondary school teaching and was well-known for his *Latin for Americans* series.
3. CJ 38 (1942-43) 184.
4. *ibid* 257-259.
5. *ibid* 513-525.
6. *ibid* 513-517.
7. *ibid* 560.
8. CJ 40 (1944-45) 513.

# S E V E N  *The Post War Period Through the 1950s*

*The old order changeth, yielding place to new, . . .*
Tennyson

THE SECOND WORLD WAR ENDED IN AUGUST 1945. As the new academic year began soon after, the world was once again at peace, although the appalling consequences of almost six years of global conflict remained, begging for solutions. The Classical Association of the Middle West and South had just celebrated its fortieth birthday; it had survived two world wars, an enormous economic dislocation, changes in educational tastes and philosophies. There must have been many members who, in the summer of 1945, felt with Horace

*Tu ne quaesieris, scire nefas, quem mihi, quem tibi*
*finem di dederint. . . .*

The Association was as ready for the new period as a body of its character could have been. By chance, a new editor for *CJ* had been appointed, who in his youth and experience, gained from a triennium of service as secretary-treasurer, was prepared to take the *Journal* in new directions. Norman J. DeWitt of Washington University, son of the president of 1938-39, introduced a new style and a new format to a publication that had remained essentially unchanged for two scores of years. The spacious type was replaced by a smaller, more compact font, the single line across the page gave way to double columns, editorials essentially ceased. This last step eliminated a regular forum wherein both officers and editors could communicate with the members of the Association and the wider readership on various matters of importance. The number of annual issues was reduced from nine to eight, the number of pages in each from sixty-four to forty-eight, with the exception of one larger number, so that the total number of pages in volume forty-one was 400 rather than 576. Yet, in spite of this reduction, more material was published, with a total of some 290,000 words against the earlier 230,000.

Both membership in the Association and subscriptions to *CJ* rose. But financial difficulties remained, with the result that membership fees and the subscription rate were increased, with effect for the 1947-48 year.

The meeting in Cincinnati, which had been cancelled the year before, was now held, with much the same program as had been originally announced. Perhaps its chief feature now, however, was a Panel Discussion on "What Can We Learn from the Army Area and Language Study Program?" This subject forecast what would be the Association's chief concern over the next several years, the instruction of Latin in the schools. The main question was, how can the early years of Latin study be made more attractive, so that those who would take only two years would be attracted rather than repelled. Caesar's primacy in the second year faced a strong challenge.

This "Project," under the jurisdiction of the Committee on Educational

Policies, consumed a large part of the Association's energies. The driving force behind it was Dr. Lenore Geweke, who enlisted a substantial number of colleagues to aid the enterprise. At the Nashville meeting of 1947, the Committee sponsored a session on "The Improvement of Latin Instruction in the First Two Years of High School," which formed the basis of a Report published at CJ 43 (1947-48) 67-90, entitled "Toward Improvement of the High-School Latin Curriculum." At the next meeting in Milwaukee, there was a second session devoted to the high school curriculum, focusing on the formulation of a two-year Latin program based upon Vergil. These deliberations were also published the following year, under the title "Toward Improvement of the High-School Latin Curriculum II," CJ 44 (1948-49) 97-143. This undertaking attracted wide-spread interest and a good deal of enthusiasm. The American Council of Learned Societies awarded the Committee a grant of $7500 in its support.

Indeed, if mention in a national newsmagazine is considered one of the peaks of success for such an educational undertaking, the "Vergil in the Second Year Project" was eminently successful. TIME Magazine devoted a full page to it in the August 16, 1948, issue. Classics, for the first time in quite some years, could enjoy good news in the public arena.

**Arma Virumque...**

For Julius Caesar, another Ides of March was ahead, though this time the main conspirator looked more like Fanny Farmer than Cassius. She is a serious Midwestern schoolmarm, with a bent for poetry, baking cakes, and putting in a garden. But if Miss Lenore Geweke (pronounced gave-a-key) has her way—and she well might—Latin beginners all over the U.S. will no longer fight their way through Caesar's trim, tight prose.

Miss Geweke began plotting more than ten years ago, and has already won some powerful support. With a Ph.D. in the classics, and years of Latin teaching behind her, she had seen too many school kids make hard going of Caesar's *Gallic War*. When they finished at the end of the second year of Latin, most of them usually dropped Latin forever. Miss Geweke's plan: if most schoolkids are only going to take two years of Latin, why not give them "the best Latin"? Why not give them Vergil and his *Aeneid*?

**More Glamor.** To many an old-school Latin teacher, the idea was heresy. Vergil, they said, was much too difficult, too full of poet's irregularities. Besides, boys at least, liked to read about wars. Rubbish, said Miss Geweke. There was adventure and glamor in the *Aeneid* ("It contains an exciting love affair"). It was a masterpiece, "the most balanced work in all Latin literature." And it was certainly no harder than Caesar, with his long, closely knit sentences, his use of subjunctives, indirect discourse and the historical present. The Classical Association of the Middle West and South (she is chairman of its educational policies committee) backed her up, and the American Council of Learned Societies gave her $7,500 to prove her point.

Last week, in a book-littered room on the University of Chicago campus, Miss Geweke was buried in vocabulary and syntax. She had three scholars working with her; volunteers in schools and colleges all over the U.S. had answered her discreet little notes asking for help, placed in classical journals. A professor at Tulane University had made her a list of 8,000 Latin words which closely resemble the English. A teacher at Pennsylvania's Ursinus College had made a frequency count of Vergil's vocabulary. The chairman of the State University of Iowa's classics department, one of her associates, had made a frequency count of syntax forms. Miss Geweke had begun to write the lessons that would best prepare pupils for Vergil. She had hoped to try out her theories in 30 public and private school systems, has already found 52 willing to try it.

**Less Grammar.** Miss Geweke and Co. think that grammar should not be taught as if pupils were ever going to speak or teach Latin. She hopes to start pupils reading as soon as possible. In the first year they can learn enough grammar to read Vergil, she thinks, without parsing, and without memorizing the declension of every noun or the conjugation of every verb. They will learn each case "across the board" for nouns of all declensions, rather than all cases for each word. She and her associates have also combined ten types of genitives (measure, quality, possession, etc.) into two basic types, 17 ablatives into three. The important thing, says Miss Geweke, is for beginning pupils to learn to read Latin with understanding and pleasure. Cicero and Caesar, and the additional grammar to understand them, would come in advanced courses.

But even if her experiments succeed (Vergil will get about a four-year try), she will still have a fight on her hands in one section of the U.S. The Classical Association of the Atlantic States is still unwilling to render unto Vergil the things that are Caesar's. Says Miss Geweke: "We're not trying to disparage Caesar. We just think that Vergil is better."

Courtesy of *TIME*, Copyright Time, Inc., 1948. (August 16, 1948)[1]

There were other innovations and successes during these years. Volume 42 of the *Journal* contained some eighty-five pages of archaeological material provided by the Archaeological Institute of America, following an agreement between the two organizations so that archaeological discoveries and insights could be brought to the attention of a wider audience than that found by the *American Journal of Archaeology*. The Association's attempt to establish a similar arrangement with The American Philological Association, for the wider dissemination of philological research, had equal success. The first of a series of articles to be published under the auspices of the APA's Committee for the Diffusion of Philological Knowledge appeared in the April 1949 number of *CJ*.[2] The author was Charles Alexander Robinson, Jr., the title "The Greeks in the Far East." The articles were intended to cover a very wide range of topics, literary, historical, and philological; their purpose was to present some of the findings and problems of scholarship to a larger classical audience. They themselves would give evidence of the broad scope of modern classical scholarship.

A new constitution was prepared in 1947, attendance at the 1948 meeting reached above 370 persons, the Semple Award for study in Rome during the summer was awarded for the first time, and a Greek Scholarship to be awarded to an undergraduate was established through the generosity of an anonymous donor. Membership stabilized in the 2100 range before rising above 2300 in 1949-50 and the Association's finances improved.

At the Richmond meeting of 1949, the feature of the program occurred after the banquet, when seven speakers, covering all the states of CAMWS's territory, offered "A Tribute to Past Leaders in Classical Scholarship."

The Association "Incorporated" under the laws of the State of Missouri as of June 10, 1948. This step established CAMWS as a legal entity in perpetuity, assuring possible benefactors of tax exemption benefits and freeing officers from liability to legal action as individuals. The Executive Committee held an *extra ordinem* meeting in St. Louis on December 30, 1948, in conjunction with the APA meeting, the first Executive Committee gathering since incorporation.

The year 1949-50 saw the third woman president, Mary V. Braginton, and two innovations which have long since become parts of the Association's *mores maiorum*. At the annual meeting, a registration fee was charged and Latin *Ovationes*, honoring distinguished members of the Association, were prepared and delivered by William C. Korfmacher.

For eight years, the Association had profited from the close proximity of the Secretary-Treasurer and the Editor. From 1942 to 1945, DeWitt and Tavenner were members of the same department at Washington University, with adjoining offices. The savings in time and postage from this close relationship were substantial; difficulties could be immediately solved. When DeWitt became Editor and Korfmacher succeeded him as Secretary-Treasurer, they were both in the same city, St. Louis, always accessible to each other by means of a local phone call. In the early 1950s this ended, as first DeWitt and then Korfmacher concluded their terms of service. Circumstances changed dramatically. The new editor was Clyde Murley of Northwestern, whose Herculean task was made even more difficult by the lack of secretarial assistance or any relief from his teaching or other academic duties. There was also a new printer with a new method of publication. The result was a series of delays, to which many members responded acrimoniously. One consequence was cancellation of memberships. During the year the number of members dropped by some twenty per cent, to 1869, to which an increase in dues contributed, thereby further damaging the already parlous finances of the Association. A vicious cycle had begun, with the Association becoming weaker and smaller and the *Journal* less appealing and reliable. The Editor asked for understanding in a brief note in his first issue:

Ed. Note: "A policy," Kipling wrote, "is blackmail levied on the fool by the unforeseen." Previous editors have realized that the *Journal* was apt to be thought too little erudite by scholars, too much so by school-teachers; to fall between two stools, not quite satisfying either group. Much has been done, as in the scholarly but non-technical papers provided by the APA committee, to relieve this situation; but the problem will persist. An editor would like to obey Horace: *Denique sit quod vis, simplex dumtaxat et unum.*

Some mutual forbearance is called for. Professors will have to remember that their destinies are tied up with the high school situation, and be tolerant of discussion of methods and curricular matters which, under ideal educational conditions, we might be glad to fore-go. Pupils are expected in many school systems to learn without studying. Some three-fourths of the subscribers are secondary school teachers. The latter, some of whom themselves have considerable attainments, will not expect scholars to be satisfied with only an exchange of class-room devices; and will welcome intellectual stimulus. You are invited to write in what you do or do not like about the *Journal*, and what you would like. The editor cannot guarantee to answer such letters (or not to); but please indicate whether you are willing to be quoted, fully or in excerpts, for there may be a column for that.

It is not to be assumed by readers or my predecessor (should he subscribe) that any changes, any deviations from the Norm, reflect on previous practice; they may be owing to financial or other exigency. What with inexperience, loss of the invaluable aid of the assistant editor (though he and his superior were most generous), the absence of others of the staff in summer and my absence from my own desk—if this first issue is mechanically passable, it will be by the grace of God and the Banta Publishing Company. As for the content, the transfer of a so-called back-log (but immune to combustion) of sixty-odd accepted MSS, not to mention book-reviews, will for some time protect readers from my judgment. The reviews are being printed in order of dates of publication of the books; the need of balancing issues, and the needs of secondary school teachers, will not allow so simple an order always for articles. Any editorial page has been, for the present, omitted in the interest of such contributors.[3]

The annual meeting in Memphis had as its feature a symposium entitled "The Classical Tradition Lives," with four speakers whose subjects were Architecture, Art, English Literature, and American Literature.

Continuing the Association's concern with teaching, there was a Panel Discussion on the subject, *Quem ad Finem Doces?*

With this meeting Korfmacher vacated the Secretary-Treasurership and was succeeded by John Hough of the University of Colorado. The cost of transferring the Association's records and equipment from St. Louis to Boulder strained finances further. Then, in the middle of the year, Hough took up appointment as a Fulbright Visiting Professor in Australia and was absent from February 1, 1952, to February 1, 1953. Establishment of smooth functioning of the office in Boulder was further hindered "by the necessity of obtaining a new assistant twice the month previous to the departure of the Secretary-Treasurer. (Acts of God and the Draft Board compelled these unexpected changes.)" [4]

During the year, Hough had warned the members of the Executive Committee of CAMWS's serious financial plight and had offered recommendations for severe economies. This led to drastic retrenchments in *CJ*. Murley reported to the Executive Committee what steps he had taken. "He informed the Committee that his plan to make financial retrenchments by omitting one or more issues, or by combining two issues, in the present volume of *CJ* had been vetoed by the postal authorities. He was then forced to plan some issues of a reduced size. He explained the technical reasons for the grievous delay on the part of the printer. He mentioned that an unwelcome method of financial retrenchments had been adopted, in the cessation of the practice of giving free reprints to authors. To relieve himself of part of the burden he is carrying, he is trying to get a volunteer advertising manager and expects to have some stenographic help by a student."[5] As a result, the first four issues of volume 47 had, successively, 60, 48, 32, and 16 pages, while the final four each had 48, the total being 348, much the smallest since the first years of the *Journal's* existence.

These financial and personnel problems entirely overshadowed the first Canadian meeting in the Association's history. Toronto in April offered a glorious welcome, but registration was low, only a bit above one hundred, who were further disheartened by the Secretary's report that the membership had fallen to 1385, down 488 from the previous year. There was, however, one thin silver lining in this gloomy cloud; the current figure contained no delinquent members, whereas earlier figures had continued to report such persons as active.

Difficulties with the *Journal* continued into the next year. There were once again long delays in its appearance, and, although the individual issues did not vary as much as in the previous volume, the total of pages was again reduced, dropping to 320, with the smallest offering twenty-four. Membership similarly continued to drop, falling below 1300. The only cheering event was the full capitalization and investment of the Semple Fund.

The year 1953-54 saw a change in fortunes. It was to see the fiftieth anniversary meeting, to be held in one of the Association's birthplaces. A committee had, for several years, been planning for the festive occasion. The general mood was in keeping with celebration; membership rose somewhat, the *Journal* was appearing regularly, with seven issues of forty-eight pages each and one of forty-four, and the Association's cash balance rose modestly. The highlight of the meeting was the program following the banquet, when W. L. Carr spoke on the Association's first fifty years,[6] Paul L. MacKendrick looked ahead to the next fifty, and the editor discussed the *Classical Journal.*[7] MacKendrick's address, in epic form with his accustomed wit and verve, merits presentation in full:

## THE NEXT FIFTY YEARS

Greetings from the APA

MY FIRST and pleasant task this April day
Is bringing greetings from the APA,
A parent spry who loves at 85
To see a 50-year-old daughter thrive,
Who wished you well to start with, in '04,
And sends me here to wish you centuries more,
Growing in wisdom and in influence,
To teach our brash compatriots common-sense;
By precept and example demonstrating
The classics well deserve their past high rating.
A symbol of our solidarity,
The *Guidance Pamphlet*'s here for all to see,
And our cooperation's in fine feather,
Wherever school and college get together,
And teachers learn from shared experience,
The grass is green on both sides of the fence.
We meet at times like these to pool our knowledge,
And prove there is no gulf 'twixt school and college.
From APA best wishes I express
To all our friends in CAMWS.

MUSE, MY PEN with poesy inspire,
The while into the future I enquire.
Remove the cloud from round the crystal ball,
The while, at the Association's call,
I peer into the darkness of the years,
And prophesy a prospect without tears:
Classrooms a-bulge with eager faces bright,
All well prepared, competing to recite.
Nouns they decline with horizontal zeal,
Before Word-Order they no terrors feel.
No longer squirms beneath our eye the dunce:
He conjugates his verb-forms all at once.
Within six weeks, full of desire to please,

Our young translate the *Metamorphoses*.
And over all, benign, with fame repleat,
There beams the modest face of WALDO SWEET.
His left hand tapes, his right a record holds,
About his neck a film strip falls in folds.
His be the glory now that never fades:
His Latin's hot with audio-visual aids.

THE CRYSTAL BALL yields next a summer scene,
With youths and maidens sporting on the green.
The campus swarms with Latin teachers gay,
At Indiana and at Iowa.
At Minnesota's door the hordes descend
And toward Wisconsin one discerns a trend.
At Michigan, Ohio, Illinois
The teachers in their thousands now deploy.
"Why are they there?" you ask? The answer's plain.
For summer WORKSHOP time is come again.
Throughout the land, in laboratory session,
One teacher hymns the Latin Week procession,
Another tells what "Latin Banquet" means:
Freshmen in sheets, devouring pork and beans,
And uttering deathless Ciceronian prose,
As out of Dixie cups the grape juice flows;
A third recounts the triumph of her day:
'Tis Arthur Godfrey as a Latin play.
A fourth is twittering like a flock of linnets:
Her class learned all its forms in twenty minutes.
Professor X next dominates the stage,
Deplores the fripperies of this sorry age
In which the way to Fame's not far to seek:
It is to know no Latin and less Greek.
His lecture still has its full hour to run:
He spends it proving Latin can be fun
By citing endless tomes in French and German
To show how Plautus outranks Ethel Merman.
And having filled—and overflowed—his hour.
He reascends into his Ivory Tower,
And leaves it to the teachers to mull over
How soph'mores take to Pauly and Wissowa.

ANOTHER PROSPECT now its head doth rear:
Its name is "Latin for the Second Year".
The tyranny of Caesar's at an end:
It seems as though he never had a friend.
His charm of style completely now has missed us
And no one dreams of mentioning Ariovistus.

Instead, the martial gauntlet down is thrown
By loud contenders for great Caesar's throne.
Here we have Vergil. Downcast he of mien
At thoughts of how he'll look to age thirteen.
Here Ovid struts, anticipating laurels
For all that he can do for 'teen-age morals.
A vapid smile enwreathes EUTROPIUS' face:
A second-rater in a champion's place,
But in the background of the crystal ball
We see that Caesar's winning after all.

TO GRADE-SCHOOL now we shift our seer's gaze,
Where foreign language teaching is the craze.
Here French we find is taking quite a beating
From students from irregular verbs retreating.
For nine-year olds this tongue has had its day:
They're bored to tears by *"Parlez-vous francais?"*
The fourth grade says it does not care at all,
To lisp, Castilian, "Habla Usted Espanol?"
In vain the German teachers nod and beckon:
The fifth grade *hat kein Wollen deutsch zu sprechen.*
The Renaissance this time has come to stay,
And shavers plead for Latin every day.
Their knowledge of the syntax may be creaky,
But six-year olds lisp "Veni, vidi, vici!"

THE FUTURE promises much proliferation
For courses in the Classics in Translation.
For though in youth for Latin boys are keen
They lose the knack before they turn eighteen.
And so the college teacher earns his pay
By teaching Greek Athletics every day.
(No knowledge of the language is required.)
So football players come, if not too tired.
The thirst for culture Dr. Y assuages
By teaching Latin roots to Commerce majors.
Vulgarization earns him his just due:
To teach real Latin to the favored few.
Analogy 'twixt Then and Now he draws
And plays the gallery for its loud guffaws,
Then salves his conscience without more ado
By teaching Plato to a class of two.

ANOTHER FIELD reveals some progress made,
In fifty years of preaching to the trade
Of guidance counsellors in serried ranks
Preparing youth to work in stores and banks.

No longer do they scorn the classic tongue
In giving counsel to the callow young.
Instead, four years they constantly advise
With more in college for the very wise.
To find the cause we need not seek so far:
They all have read the pamphlet writ by CARR;
And, more than this, those who our youngsters guide
Now to a man teach Latin on the side.
No shyness now is Latin teacher's sin:
She'd learned techniques of boring from within.
(In '54 all boredom was abolished,
And youth became incredibly more polished.)

THE TALE OF WONDERS still remains untold:
For princ'pals will in future be less bold,
And superintendents foster Latin studies
And swap good Latin tags with all their buddies.
The lion with the lamb will lie at ease
In fond discourse of Latin's subtleties;
For chief among them rank the Latin teachers,
No longer now the lowliest of God's creatures.
In school-boards men will firmly pound the table
And make us teach more Latin than we're able,
And gym and band will popularity lose
The while the team courts the Vergilian Muse.
From these the teachers will receive warm greetings,
And have expenses paid to all the meetings.
Their salary scale will touch the dizziest heights,
They'll hold the stage at Parent-Teacher Nights.
The board will pay their way to Rome and Venice,
They'll show their slides to Rotary and Kiwanis.

PRESTIGE, my friends, prestige is what we're lacking,
But fifty years will send the scoffers packing,
Until the land's abloom with Latin schools
And students flock to Latin without rules.
The fame of Course in Relaxation fades
And books are hailed as audio-visual aids.

FOR EDUCATIONISTS will see the light,
And grant pre-eminence that's ours by right.
"Latin for Citizenship" is next ensuing:
With Latin we shall learn to do by doing.
And in the age of streamlined toys in plastics,
There's merit still in Caesar's bridge in matchsticks.
No longer will our subject meet derision,
When folk see "War in Gaul" on television.

THE CRYSTAL BALL clouds over. Fancy's play
Is ended, and we face the light of day,
Knowing that what will make the dream come true
Is faith, and work, and propaganda too.
We'll meet the opposition, yes, and sink it
If we remember LABOR OMNIA VINCIT. [8]

The program offered another novelty, a joint session on the Friday evening with the St. Louis Society of the Archaeological Institute of America and Eta Sigma Phi, at which the speaker was the President of the Institute, Henry T. Rowell of The Johns Hopkins University.

There were two major changes in the activities and procedures of the Association. Amendments to the Constitution were approved, which established the office of President-Elect and added the designee to the Executive Committee. Henceforth, the Association would select an individual who would then proceed, the following year, directly to the presidency. This change meant that the new president would have a year of participation on the Committee and would not come to office without being fully aware of the Association's activities. The Delcamp Greek award was discontinued at the end of 1953.

At the conclusion of the next year *CJ* underwent another change at its helm. Murley resigned the editorship as he became emeritus at Northwestern in August 1955. He died in April 1957; I have learned from one of his colleagues and friends, *per litteras*, that the heavy burdens of the *Journal* and the distress and anguish which it brought upon him unquestionably hastened his death.[9]

Phillip De Lacy of Washington University was designated Acting Editor for one year, with Norman T. Pratt of Indiana University to assume the office as of spring semester 1956. With the completion of fifty volumes, an Index to cover volumes 26-50 was approved.

The second half of the decade brought welcome routine. The Association experienced steady growth, with membership rising to almost 2200 and subscribers to *CJ* to 4363 in 1960. There were, however, very few new initiatives or major undertakings. The period was one of recovery and consolidation. Highlights were sparse.

The February 1956 issue of *Classical Journal* commemorated the fiftieth anniversary of The Classical Association of New England. Guest editor was Sterling Dow of Harvard University, whose editorial remarks recalled the common origins of all American regional classical organizations.

> It is a pleasure and an honor to acknowledge, on behalf of the Classical Association of New England, the greetings of its three sister organizations. Their kindness is appreciated. When CANE meets this April in Concord, we shall hope to welcome, and to thank again, representatives of CAAS, CAMWS, and CAPS. The four organizations were founded in the same period, and the semi-centennial of one is a fitting occasion to recall the

extraordinary unity and unanimity of all four, a happy manifestation of Classical universality.

Two of the organizations have no publication of their own, and it is a special kindness of CAMWS, here acknowledged with hearty gratitude, to have given to its destitute sister this issue of *The Classical Journal.* The regular Editor deserves special thanks for his patience, and the Guest Editor is only too well aware that the readers also, deprived of all their regular departments, may need to exercise patience until their New England guest, with her unfamiliar ways in these pages, is gone.[10]

The annual meeting in Lexington had two highlights, a Panel Discussion on "The Content of Second-Year Latin" and a Symposium on "Linguistics and the Classical Languages." In 1957 Professor Pratt published a brief editorial which well expressed the improved state of the classics combined with lingering uncertainty.

Too Many Groans?

The only criticism *expressed* during the Editor's first year came from a gentleman who asked why authors in *CJ* kept writing about the "decline" of our subject, while his enrollment has been increasing steadily up to a very substantial size; he proved his point by submitting figures to The Forum. Our colleague is right; we probably have been overindulging in lamentation. What is more, during the year we have heard much more optimistic sounds coursing through the pages. The Editor's *personal* view is that the worst of the depression is behind us, but that obviously we are still some reach away from the position which our field should occupy. Whether this gap will be closed depends largely on whether we succeed in recruiting superior candidates for all levels of our work. Those who are responsible for hiring new college Classics teachers know that we have right now a shortage at this level comparable to the dearth for the secondary schools. We have barely begun to impress this upon the general public. There is no reason now not to encourage all who promise success. Solution will require a prodigious effort.[11]

Unexpected difficulties would soon arise. Later this year, in October 1957, the Soviet Union placed Sputnik in orbit. The devastating effects upon American morale were immediate; the effects upon the American educational system and its sense of values did not come as quickly. Even "a prodigious effort" on the part of Classicists would not suffice.

In 1958 the Association met in Austin, its first gathering in the state, although the Southern Section had gone to San Antonio in 1939. The following year saw a return to Milwaukee, where the registration reached 261, the highest since the last meeting in this city, in 1948. During the year a new standing committee was appointed, the Committee on Merit.

Its first action is to regularize as a tradition the recent practice at the annual dinner of presenting *ovationes* of distinguished persons, usually *seniores* of CAMWS and often such *seniores* belonging to the general locale of the meeting; on occasion, this honor has been accorded persons outside the Association. It has also been agreed that these *ovationes* should receive public notice through publication in CJ. [12]

The presentation of these *ovationes* has proven to be one of the highlights of the annual gatherings.

The first meeting of the new decade, in April 1960, took place in Athens, Georgia. As indicated earlier, the report on the Association's membership and finances was optimistic. The most prominent part of the program was a Panel Discussion on the "Recruitment and Preparation of Latin Teachers for Secondary Schools." [13] But no one at that meeting could possibly have, in the wildest fantasy, foreseen some of the events that the sixties would witness: the election and assassination of President Kennedy, the elimination of Latin in the Mass by Vatican Council II, the escalation of the Vietnam War, the Cuban crisis, the space race, the civil rights movement, the assassinations of Dr. King and Senator Kennedy. All changed the character of society, with ever increasing anti-intellectualism. Education could not avoid the fallout; classics would suffer another depression, as it had after the first world war. Survival was once again to become the prime issue.

## NOTES

1. CJ 44 (1948-49) 95.
2. *ibid* 405-412.
3. CJ 46 (1950-51) 4.
4. Secretary's Report, April 1952, Paragraph 5.
5. Executive Committee Minutes, April 1952, Paragraph 9.
6. CJ 50 (1954-55) 195-199.
7. *ibid* 200.
8. *ibid* 201-204.
9. An obituary notice appeared at CJ 53 (1957-58) 222.
10. CJ 51 (1955-56) 195.
11. CJ 52 (1956-57) 358.
12. CJ 54 (1958-59) 239.
13. The four papers, by Paul MacKendrick, Gertrude Ewing, Joseph Conant, and Lucy Robertson, appeared at CJ 56 (1960-61) 203-210.

# EIGHT *The Decades of the 1960s and 1970s*

IN 1960 THERE WERE 654,670 STUDENTS enrolled in high school Latin study. Two years later, enrollment peaked at just above 700,000 students. In 1970, that figure had fallen to 265,293, in 1976 to 150,470.[1] In less than a decade and a half, the number of students studying Latin in the public high schools of the nation had fallen almost eighty per cent. The crisis of the 1920s was being played out once again, but the risk was now greater. The study of classics had always been on the defensive when questions of practicality came to the fore. Now, however, with the federal government responding to the failings of American education as evidenced by our secondary place in the space race, public monies were made available as seldom before, but the focus of attention was that broad range of disciplines which would serve the public weal. The National Defense Education Act at first expressly excluded the study of classics, and, even when the classical languages were permitted to share in the public largesse, it remained a constant challenge to show that these studies had a role to play in the present period of malaise. The Classical Association of the Middle West and South devoted a large part of its energies and resources to this struggle during the gloomy period of the 1960s.

The annual meetings frequently featured sessions concerned with teaching in the schools and with the high school curriculum. In 1961, there was a discussion on "Programs in the Classics for Superior High School Students," in 1962 a symposium on "Programming of Latin in the High School," in 1963 another symposium on "Methods of Teaching Latin, Old and New." In 1965 the subject was "The Articulation of the Latin Curriculum: High School to College" and in 1969 "The Expanded Curriculum: Latin in Grades 7 through 12." Further, in order to induce capable high school students of Latin to continue their study in college, the Association instituted, effective with the academic year 1963-64, a program of scholarships (the name was subsequently changed to awards) for youngsters resident in the area of the Association.

The chief response to the ever increasing difficulties was the establishment of an umbrella organization named CAUSA (Classical Associations USA). The person largely responsible was John F. Latimer, the president of the American Classical League. The purposes and goals of the new organization were amply set forth in *The Classical World*, almost entirely in Latimer's own words.

## CAUSA

Members and friends of CAAS planning to attend the Association's annual spring meeting at Goucher College, April 24 and 25, will be privileged to hear, as a major feature of the distinguished program already announced, Professor John F. Latimer's personal *suasio* of perhaps the most important single issue before the classical community today. We are happy to be able to present to our readers at this time a briefing, as far as possible in Professor Latimer's own words, on the original concept of CAUSA; a progress report; and finally—and entirely on our own editorial responsibility—our personal estimate of the significance of Professor Latimer's plea to the profession.

We take the welcome opportunity, then, of quoting first from a MEMORANDUM TO THE PRESIDENTS OF AIA, APA, CAAS, CAMWS, CANE, CAPS, ETA SIGMA PHI, issued by Professor Latimer, in his capacity as President of ACL, on July 18, 1963. Professor Latimer began (in the following we have omitted for reasons of space some illustrative and historical detail presented by the writer):

I suggest that the time has come to consider carefully the formation of a committee to coordinate the various classical activities in this country. I believe that unified action is needed to

1. Organize a national campaign to attract former Latin teachers into the schools and to alert secondary and college students to the great need and opportunity for Latin teachers throughout the United States.
2. Organize Workshops for Latin teachers in geographical areas where no such educational facilities are available or planned.
3. Expand the teacher placement services provided by ACL, APA, and CAAS, and the work of ACL's Service Bureau.
4. Promote and organize "Laymen for Latin" Clubs on local and state levels, and possibly national.
5. Set up teacher qualifications at various levels.
6. Develop and refine teaching aids and methods and make them widely known and available.
7. Promote Advanced Placement for Latin and, as appropriate, Greek students.
8. Promote the study of Greek in secondary schools and in colleges.
9. Organize programs comparable to Junior Year Abroad and Summer Study for high school and college students.
10. Present a united front in recommending and supporting congressional and state legislation affecting education in this country.

Professor Latimer continued:

To accomplish these and other desirable goals, it is proposed that a coordinating committee be formed consisting of one or two representatives from each of the addressee organizations and ACL. The Committee, composed of representatives of classical associations of the USA, might fittingly be called CAUSA. Chairman of CAUSA would be an Executive Secretary, employed full time with funds provided by payment of one dollar additional annual dues from each member of the constituent associations. Members with more than one affiliation would pay the fee only once. CAUSA would act in an advisory capacity to the Executive Secretary, who would carry out the program determined by CAUSA. The ten items listed above constitute merely a suggestive tentative program.

It is thought that each of the constituent associations would maintain its own identity, officers, and publications. Each would hold its regular stated meetings and programs. CAUSA might periodically issue an information sheet to all of the constituent membership.

It is believed that cooperative action of this kind would make it feasible to approach one of the foundations for funds to support a national enterprise of this nature.

The Memorandum concluded with a request to the several Presidents to come or to send representatives to a proposed meeting in Washington, October 19-20, 1963, "for an exchange of ideas" on the suggested plan of action.

The immediate response to the call spoke well, we should say, both for the timeliness of Professor Latimer's action and the alertness of the *summi magistratus*. Representatives of seven of the eight societies met at the Cosmos Club in Washington, October 19, 1963. A second Memorandum, over date of October 22, 1963, reports that after "wide-ranging discussion extending from lunch through the afternoon and into the evening":

It was the consensus of the group that the proper role of the Classics in the education of American youth was a matter that challenged the best efforts of secondary school and college teachers and demanded the highest form of cooperation. To enable the Classics to regain and perform their educational role most effectively today two basic needs were deemed critically urgent: *Revision of the secondary school curriculum* and *recruitment and training of teachers*. [Italics ours.]

Hundreds of individual teachers throughout the country are doing outstanding work in the classroom. Many Latin programs, however, are suffering from poorly prepared instructors; many have been curtailed or dropped for the mere lack of teachers. Good teachers are often handicapped by textbooks that fail to stimulate and hold the interest of intelligent students for whom the study of Latin could be made an exciting and rewarding experience in the humanities.

These are oft-told tales. They are briefly cited here to underscore the concern with which your representatives view the current situation. The crux of the matter, in our opinion, lies in the secondary school. What happens in and at that level has a direct up-and-down relationship with what happens in the college. Many colleges do a magnificent job of educating Latin teachers for the schools. But all too prevalent is the lack of communication between the college or university classical scholar and the secondary school classical teacher. The point and the results do not need to be labored.

Concerted action on these and related problems is long overdue. Cooperative ventures have been undertaken in the past and individual organizations have tried and are trying to resolve some of the issues involved. But the urgency and magnitude of the remedies needed cry out for more direct and united efforts. To that end, taking a leaf from MLA's book—historians and mathematicians have not too long since done the same—the Ad Hoc Committee recommends that the four national organizations and the four regional associations form a classical federation to be known as CAUSA, with each of the constituent bodies "maintaining its own identity, officers and publications. Each would hold its regular stated meeting and programs..." To formulate the plans, policies and activities of CAUSA, each of the constituent bodies would elect one representative and one alternate for three-year terms. These representatives would constitute the "governing committee" which for convenience, would be called "CAUSA." To serve as its administrative head the governing committee, each with votes proportionate to the constituent body's membership, would elect a full time Executive Secretary.

Partial funds for CAUSA's budget would be provided by annual payment from each of the four regional associations and ACL to the amount of $1 for each of its members (by the institution of a membership fee of $1, it is suggested, or by the addition of $1 to the membership fee). AIA, APA, and Eta Sigma Phi, because of their differing circumstances, would make appropriate annual contributions. It is estimated that $10,500 would be raised annually by the first method, and $1,500 by the second.

It is obvious that $12,000 would not be enough to secure a competent full time Executive Secretary, to say nothing of secretarial help, office expenses, travel and the like. Several possible supplementary sources are suggested: foundation support, governmental funds, and JCL. There is little hope for the first unless we give evidence of supporting our program in a real way. The second will depend primarily on provisions of the law. The third might have tremendous potential but it should be considered only with the greatest care and reluctance.

The Ad Hoc Committee was not empowered to establish CAUSA. As a matter of the greatest urgency and need, however, it urges CAUSA's incipient organizational members to consider its establishment with something more than deliberate speed.

◆ ◆ ◆

*Haec hactenus.* The sequel? Pending reports of action at the various regional spring meetings, it cannot be said that, as of now, the response of the profession as a whole has been either informed or unequivocal or even indicative of any real awareness of the urgency for cooperative action with "something more than deliberate speed." To those still haunted by thoughts of the spectral "One Big Union" the results of comparable action, noted above, by MLA and by scientific bodies should be sufficient answer. The inconclusive results of CETT certainly provide no dissuasive precedent: the structural defects in that noble experiment can be eliminated in CAUSA. Above all, the new organization presents an unmatched opportunity to give the lie once and for all to the ludicrous stereotype of ours as a moribund discipline. As our published reports have shown, in grassroots organization (October), academic status (January), school (May 1961) and college (June 1962) enrollments, we assuredly *do* still matter in the educational world. Professor Latimer's proposal at last provides us with a means of exercising our latent strength in today's ruthlessly competitive educational structure.—E.A.R.[2]

To this reasoned appeal the Association responded nobly. Its membership grew and remained strong throughout the decade; numbering only 2192 in 1960, it reached 2768 in 1968 and was still above 2600 in 1970. The *Journal's* circulation followed a similar pattern, from 4363 at the beginning of the decade to a peak of 5244 in 1968, with 4816 in 1970. Beginning with the year 1965-66, the Association contributed over $11,000 to the American Classical League without restriction of use in support of its expanded work to further classical studies. As a consequence, the Association's cash balance almost disappeared, with only $347 available as of June 30, 1969. But the officers of the Association properly concluded that it would be folly to hoard the available resources against another emergency, when the present one threatened the demise of both our subjects and our organization.

Welcome support appeared late in the decade from a body which had once been considered in the enemy's camp, the champions of the modern languages.

## STATEMENT BY THE NATIONAL COUNCIL OF STATE SUPERVISORS OF FOREIGN LANGUAGES: THE ROLE OF LATIN IN AMERICAN EDUCATION

The National Council of State Supervisors of Foreign Languages endorses and encourages the teaching of Latin in American schools.

The rationale offered for Latin is essentially the same as that for the modern languages; through the study of a foreign language the monocultural and monolingual individual expands the boundaries of his own relatively narrow world to circumscribe a world which is at once more cosmopolitan. It is this very fact of foreign language study which makes languages crucial to the humanities.

Yet the continuing value of Latin to today's curriculum rests in its *uniqueness*. Latin presents the student an opportunity to develop a sense of the significant past by coming into direct contact with the Roman world. The late William Riley Parker, Distinguished Service Professor of English at Indiana University, said: "To live intellectually *only in one's own time is as* provincial and misleading as to live intellectually *only in one's own culture.*" The importance of the past from which all Western civilization has evolved is self-evident.

That Latin differs in its grammar from most languages commonly taught in our schools—even radically in the case of English—illustrates again the unique contribution this ancient language can make. Since Latin is one of the highly inflected languages, its contrast with English is especially sharp. The potential of Latin to create general linguistic concepts within the speaker of English makes it an ideal instrument for developing a deeper understanding of language *per se*.

As a means of building an historical perspective, of developing linguistic concepts, of creating a sense of judgment based on understanding of the past, Latin remains unsurpassed.

Although benefits do accrue from even a brief encounter with a foreign language, it is generally recognized that language competence results from extended sequences of study. The values of the study of Latin outlined here assume that a person will have the opportunity to pursue his study for three to six years.

Multi-sensory methods and materials especially suited to the interests, needs, and abilities of secondary-school students can make the teaching of Latin more meaningful than using a traditional approach at these levels.

As modern languages move on the educational spectrum into the elementary and junior high schools, the number of youngsters studying two or more languages becomes increasingly widespread.

The Council urges educators to reassess the values of Latin to the curriculum. The continuing decrease of Latin enrollments in the schools is alarming to many. This decrease can most readily be attributed to the small number of Latin teachers being prepared by colleges and universities; retirement of the Latin teacher sometimes means dropping Latin from the curriculum.

The Council encourages the American Classical League in its efforts toward developing standards for teacher education in Latin and disseminating information about new methods and materials in the teaching of Latin. Latin teachers and their modern-foreign-language colleagues realize that the value of any foreign language study is, in the final analysis, directly dependent upon the effectiveness of their teaching.[3]

larity. But it became increasingly evident that the strain of publishing eight numbers during an academic year was greater than an editor and his staff could bear. W. R. Jones died suddenly during the summer of 1968; two years later, the decision was reached to publish the *Journal* in four issues of ninety-six pages each, beginning with volume 66, 1970-71. In this retreat to a saner printing schedule, the Association followed, at a distance of thirteen years, the precedent of its sister publication, *The Classical Weekly*, which, in 1957, had moved from sixteen issues during the academic year to eight, from what had been essentially a bi-weekly publication to a monthly, and, with that, had changed its name to *The Classical World.*

The need of the secondary school teacher for experiencing the classical lands in person remained one of the Association's chief concerns. Beginning in 1965, thanks to an anonymous gift to the Semple Scholarship fund and with some of the Association's own resources, three teachers were enabled annually to attend classical summer programs abroad: at the American School of Classical Studies in Athens, at the American Academy in Rome, and at the Vergilian Society's program at Cumae and on its classical tour.

As the 1970s began, the Association's programs continued to function smoothly. In 1971, Manitoba became the thirty-second regional unit, the second Canadian province to join the Association. This was the first expansion in almost fifty years. Membership and circulation stayed at satisfactorily high levels for a couple of years, and the cash balance increased substantially, making the prospects for further support of both high school student and teacher very good. But then disaster struck; the schedule of *CJ* was thrown into turmoil; a change of printer which followed appointment of a new editor caused extraordinary difficulties and delays. Volumes 67 and 68 appeared only erratically, with great intervals between numbers. This sorry state caused an enormous expenditure of energy for editor and officers, with a tremendous increase in correspondence and numerous cancellations of membership and subscription. As of July 1, 1975, five numbers remained wholly or in part undelivered from the 1971-72 and 1972-73 volumes, and one of them, the last of volume 68, had not yet been printed. This issue, when at the last it appeared, had been printed in insufficient numbers, so that in 1977 six hundred additional copies needed to be reprinted. These were finally mailed during the autumn. The chaos of missing issues, which had plagued the classical profession and librarians and had brought the Association much ill will, was finally settled. Paradoxically, in 1976 the subscription list had risen for the first time since 1968, but then the decrease continued, so that membership and subscription figures were only 1618 and 2915 respectively in 1980. The loss of membership income combined with large additional unexpected expenses strained the Association's resources dramatically. What it could do for classics and its members was sharply reduced.

In 1972, the Latin Week Committee, which for many years had made materials available for the celebration of Latin Week in high schools and communities throughout the country, came to the end of its labors, since demand for its services had dwindled greatly. Two years later, in response to the financial difficulties discussed above, the Executive Committee moved to reduce the number of college awards for high school students from nine to five and to fund only one Semple Scholarship. In a very rare defeat for an Executive Committee motion, this proposal was voted down on the floor of the business meeting, with the argument that the number of college awards was more important than the amount of money offered. A motion to offer six, each for a smaller amount, passed.

In 1975, the name of Yankton College appeared in the minutes of the Executive Committee for the first time. The disposition of trust funds in the College's keeping might ultimately benefit the Association. Patience was requisite. The full story of this event is the feature of the next chapter.

In 1977 the identity of the anonymous donor of the funds which had made possible a second Semple Scholarship for so many years was revealed, and this scholarship designated by her name. Mary A. Grant now enjoyed the kudos merited by her generous support of one of the Association's major programs. Simultaneously, and ironically, in consequence of new federal legislation which required foundations to distribute each year a specified part of their earnings, CAMWS faced the danger of being declared a taxable foundation, because of excessive income and security holdings. The response was simple and sensible; the dollar amounts of the Semple and Grant Scholarships and of the college awards were increased, and the Internal Revenue Service expressed its contentment with the Association's use of its non-profit funds.

During the following year, the Association established a new committee at the instance of the American Classical League, the Committee for the Promotion of Latin. This committee was to prove energetic and effective in the most important mission of the present day, bringing the erosion of high school Latin study to an end and reversing the process.[4] Good students needed to be attracted to start and continue this study, teachers needed to be trained and given the opportunity to improve their abilities. Consequently, the new monies received from an increase in dues were allotted to these goals. There would now be five $2,000 awards for teachers, twenty college awards of $500 for high school students, and a budget of $5,000 for the new committee.

As the decade came to an end, there was renewed confidence that the struggle for Latin could be won. Resources were substantially increased, the membership had essentially stabilized, things could only get better, it seemed. The beginning of the 1980s was not the best of all educational times, but a nadir had passed. *Classical Journal*, appearing regularly, represented the Association well, and had regained its position as one of the leading classical publications in the world. Those officers and members who had survived the manifold difficulties of the 1970s heaved collective sighs of relief.

NOTES
1. R. A. LaFleur and J. C. Anderson, Jr., "The ACL/UGA/NEH National Latin Institute: Retrospect and Prospect," CO 65 (1987-88) 110.
2. CW 57 (1963-64) 303-304, 329. The initials are those of the editor, Edward A. Robinson.

   Among the ACL's actions was the purchase of 10,000 reprints of William Riley Parker's "The Case for Latin," which appeared in PMLA 79, 4, part 2 (September 1964) 3-10. This powerful essay, by a distinguished Professor of English, coming from someone outside the classical field, was perhaps the most effective ammunition that the classics had. In his final footnote, Professor Parker wrote:

   "Some wondered why this piece should appear in PMLA. The Editor of PMLA invited me to write it, and reprints are available from the Modern Language Association (4 Washington Place, New York, N.Y. 10003) for all who wish to join me in getting it into the hands of those who most need to be informed and, perhaps, persuaded—guidance counsellors, school and college administrators, school boards, curriculum experts, and others. It is my earnest hope that, in this effort, teachers of English, linguistics, the modern foreign languages—indeed, all the humanities—will find common cause. My personal motive is to renew my allegiance to the humanistic tradition. The case for Latin seems to me a crux—in all senses of that word. My basic concern as an English teacher is the relation of language to wisdom. I like to believe that most members of the MLA share this concern."
3. CJ 64 (1968-69) 309-310.
4. For an account of the Committee's first year, see R. A. LaFleur, "Promoting Classics in the Middle West and South: A Preliminary Report" CJ 75 (1979-80) 324-329. In conjunction with this, see G. Lawall and J. Barthelmess, "The Role of the American Classical League in Promoting Dialogue within the Classical and Foreign Language Teaching Professions," ibid 330-334.

# NINE *The 1980s and Beyond*

THE FOCUS OF THE ASSOCIATION'S LIFE since the decade of the 1980s began has been to maintain equilibrium in its activities. The prime emphases, namely to encourage students to continue their study of Latin and to recruit, to help train, and to retain Latin teachers, were limited not by will but by the availability of resources. CAMWS is now, as I write in 1988, a much smaller organization than it was only a decade ago, and the influence of *Classical Journal*, as reflected in circulation, is down even more proportionately. The membership figure hovers in the 1600s; subscriptions continue above 2700. No longer the largest classical organization in the country, having long since fallen behind the American Classical League and the American Philological Association, CAMWS nonetheless remains much the largest of the regional organizations. Indeed, it has recently grown in the number of its constituent units, as Saskatchewan in 1986 became the third Canadian province to affiliate.

Early in the decade, finances were once again in critical straits, a difficulty immediately met by reduction of the accustomed awards. But soon the treasury became more stable, and the good works were again expanded. The Committee for the Promotion of Latin became a national leader in winning support for the study of Latin in the schools and in the recruitment of teachers. Resources increased substantially in 1985-86 "with the additional infusion of the Stewart bequest." This was the culmination of more than a decade of legal involvement, which at the end brought the Association the largest gift it had ever received.

On August 9, 1962, Ruth Reed Stewart of Yankton, South Dakota, made Yankton College of that city a major benefactor in her will. The pertinent parts thereof read as follows:

> I give, bequeath and devise all the rest, residue and remainder of my property, personal and real, of which disposition has not been hereinbefore made, and/or which shall become a part of my residuary estate by lapse or for any other reason, to Yankton College, an educational corporation, Yankton, South Dakota, for the following specified uses and purposes: The income from such residuary estate given to said Yankton College shall be used to endow and maintain, wholly or partly, a Professorship in the aforesaid Yankton College of Classical Languages and Literature. It is particularly desired by me that such income therefrom shall be used to endow and maintain, wholly or partly, such a Professorship, over and beyond what Yankton College may otherwise feel itself financially able to provide. This Professorship shall be known as the Manson A. Stewart Professorship.
>
> If Yankton College either shall be unwilling to accept my residuary estate subject to the uses and purposes set forth in

paragraph numbered Third of this Will, or if Yankton College shall cease to exist as a separate institution of like character as at present, then in either of such events, I give, bequeath and devise all the rest, residue and remainder of my property, personal and real, of which disposition has not been hereinbefore made, and/or which shall become a part of my residuary estate by lapse, or for any other reason, as follows:

a. One third thereof to The Classical Association of the Middle West and South, a corporation under the laws of the state of Missouri, 8 E. Hellems Building, University of Colorado, Boulder, Colorado; and

b. One third thereof to the University of Michigan, an educational corporation, Ann Arbor, Michigan, for the use of its Classical Department and

c. One third thereof to Grinnell College, an educational corporation, Grinnell, Iowa, for the use of its Classical Department.

Said bequests and devises are given in honor of Manson A. Stewart, and in using the same it is hoped said legatees and devisees will use the name of Manson A. Stewart.

Mrs. Stewart's deceased husband, Manson A. Stewart, had been Professor of Classical Languages at Yankton College for many years and a member of CAMWS.

About the same time, two other wills designated the College as a major beneficiary of substantial estates, with precise indication of the uses to which the monies should be put. For the better part of a decade, the College did little to satisfy the terms of the wills, and in 1972 the Administration liquidated more than $1,100,000 of the endowment to pay current debts. In May 1974, a hearing was held concerning the College's use of endowment funds. The College's President petitioned to be released from the terms of the bequests. The pertinent paragraphs follow:

8. That under the terms of the Last Will of Ruth Reed Stewart, now deceased, Yankton College was bequeathed the residue of her estate to be used to endow and maintain a Professorship of Classical Language and Literature at Yankton College and further providing that if Yankton College should be unwilling to accept this bequest subject to said uses and purposes or if Yankton College should cease to exist as a separate institution of like character as it was at the time said residuary estate was distributed, that the balance thereof should then go one-third each to the Classical Association of the Middle West and South,..; the University of Michigan at Ann Arbor, Michigan; and Grinell (sic) College at Grinell, Iowa. The Executive Committee of the Board of Trustees of Yankton College by resolution dated November 22, 1963, accepted this bequest on the terms and conditions therein contained....

9. That Yankton College has at all times since the acceptance of the bequest...made available courses in Classical Language and Literature, and has in the past and now has a Professor available and qualified to teach said courses. That for approximately ten years immediately prior to the filing of this Petition, no student at Yankton College has requested instruction in any courses in Classical Language and Literature, and it is now impracticable for Yankton College to be so restricted in the use of these funds although the College will continue to offer and make available courses in Classical Language and Literature.

Fewer than three weeks later, the College moved for dismissal of its own petition. But in February 1975, the College again petitioned for permission to spend money from the Stewart and one other trust. In March, CAMWS and the University of Michigan filed objections and affidavits against this petition. In response, the court entered a temporary order which allowed the College to expend the money in the other trust as well as one-third of the money in the Stewart trust. This one-third was the amount which could have been claimed by Grinnell College as a secondary beneficiary. Since Grinnell chose not to join the suit filed by CAMWS and Michigan, the court allowed the expenditure of what would have been its share. The remaining two-thirds of the estate were valued at just above $200,000.

The significance of this decision was that this sum was to be segregated from the College's other funds and that the principal could not be invaded. After further legal maneuvers on the College's part, CAMWS petitioned to remove Yankton College as a trustee of the Stewart trust on October 8, 1975. This petition was denied, but the College was required to file full and complete annual reports, which it failed to do by the end of the year, and it then requested a continuance.

So stood the case in early 1976. For the better part of a decade, nothing changed. Vigilance and alertness were essential. The end came suddenly and unexpectedly, when Yankton College declared bankruptcy and closed its doors on December 21, 1984. The Stewart trust was the only part of the endowment which had not been spent; it remained intact, worth $204,000, one half of which would come to the Association, the other to the Classical Studies department of the University of Michigan.

On May 7, 1985, the Attorney General of the State of South Dakota received notice of the Association's petition to authorize delivery of possession of the corpus of the Ruth Reed Stewart trust to the two beneficiaries. Among the conditions proposed the following are particularly germane:

5. That the trustees, respectively, are directed to keep intact, and suitably invested, the principle (sic) sums paid to it.

6. That the trustees, respectively, are authorized to use the income from the investment of the sum paid to it for the purpose of the trust, as heretofore found by the court.

7. That the furtherance and promotion of the classical languages and classical literature is not limited to maintenance of professorships but would also be accomplished by encouragement of participation in study of the same through awards of scholarships and acquisition of training aids and material used in teaching. That, to the extent feasible, recognition should be given to the desire of testatrix to perpetuate the name of "Manson A. Stewart" by designating any professorships established, scholarships awarded, or purchases made with proceeds of the trust by that name.

On July 25, 1985, the Association was formally appointed one of the trustees. During the following year, the sum of $102,000 was transmitted to it and duly placed in its treasury. Although final determination has not yet been made as to the precise uses to which the income will be put, the wishes of Professor Stewart's widow would at last be satisfied, that the cause of classical study be advanced in the name of her husband.

In July 1974, Brent M. Froberg of the University of South Dakota was designated to represent the Association's best interests. For more than a decade he did so, with unflagging attention. As classicists and as individuals, we owe him an enormous debt; *pro summis eius laboribus maximas ei gratias agimus.*

❖❖❖❖❖❖

More than eighty years have passed since W. G. Manly at the University of Missouri and several of his colleagues had a vision of a regional association to benefit classical studies. It not only still survives, it flourishes in many respects, and is *iuvenis* rather than *senex* in enthusiasm and imagination, in its devotion to *bonae artes* and *bona opera. Vivant studia classica, vivat Societas Classica Medio-Occidentalis et Australis.* May there be another installment of its history as the next century approaches its end.

# Appendix I

## OFFICERS AND EDITORS

### PRESIDENTS OF THE CLASSICAL ASSOCIATION
### OF THE
### MIDDLE WEST AND SOUTH

William G. Manly, University of Missouri, 1905-06
Moses S. Slaughter, University of Wisconsin, 1906-07
Edward Capps, University of Chicago, 1907-08
Arthur T. Walker, University of Kansas, 1908-09
Frederick C. Eastman, University of Iowa, 1909-10
Benjamin L. D'Ooge, Michigan State Normal College, 1910-11
Walter Miller, Tulane University, 1911-12
Grove E. Barber, University of Nebraska, 1912-13
Theodore C. Burgess, Bradley Polytechnic Institute, 1913-14
James H. Kirkland, Vanderbilt University, 1914-15
Herbert J. Barton, University of Illinois, 1915-16
John A. Scott, Northwestern University, 1916-17
Charles N. Smiley, Grinnell College, 1917-18
Campbell Bonner, University of Michigan, 1918-19
Gordon J. Laing, University of Chicago, 1919-20
Robert B. Steele, Vanderbilt University, 1920-21
Charles H. Weller, University of Iowa, 1921-22
Louis E. Lord, Oberlin College, 1922-23
Berthold L. Ullman, University of Iowa, 1923-24
Alexander L. Bondurant, University of Mississippi, 1924-25
Frank J. Miller, University of Chicago, 1925-26
Selatie E. Stout, University of Indiana, 1926-27
Charles E. Little, Peabody College for Teachers, 1927-28
Robert J. Bonner, University of Chicago, 1928-29
William J. Battle, University of Texas, 1929-30
Omera F. Long, Northwestern University, 1930-31
Lillian Gay Berry, University of Indiana, 1931-32
Roy C. Flickinger, University of Iowa, 1932-33
Gustave A. Harrer, University of North Carolina, 1933-34
Frederick W. Shipley, Washington University, 1934-35
Victor D. Hill, Ohio University, 1935-36
Charles C. Mierow, Carleton College, 1936-37

Hubert M. Poteat, Wake Forest College, 1937-38
Norman W. DeWitt, University of Toronto, 1938-39
Alfred P. Dorjahn, Northwestern University, 1939-40
Gertrude Smith, University of Chicago, 1940-41
Edward K. Turner, Emory University, 1941-42
Fred S. Dunham, University of Michigan, 1942-43
Clyde Pharr, Vanderbilt University, 1943-44
Walter R. Agard, University of Wisconsin, 1944-45
Eugene Tavenner, Washington University, 1945-46
Clyde Murley, Northwestern University, 1946-47
Dorrance S. White, University of Iowa, 1947-48
A. Pelzer Wagener, College of William and Mary, 1948-49
Mary V. Braginton, Rockford College, 1949-50
Clarence A. Forbes, Ohio State University, 1950-51
William C. Korfmacher, St. Louis University, 1951-52
Russel M. Geer, Tulane University, 1952-53
William E. Gwatkin, Jr., University of Missouri, 1953-54
Arthur H. Moser, University of Tennessee, 1954-55
Gerald Else, University of Iowa, 1955-56
Norman J. DeWitt, University of Minnesota, 1956-57
Harry J. Leon, University of Texas, 1957-58
Oscar E. Nybakken, University of Iowa, 1958-59
Graydon W. Regenos, Tulane University, 1959-60
John N. Hough, University of Colorado, 1960-61
Bert H. Narveson, St. Olaf College, 1961-62
Chauncey E. Finch, St. Louis University, 1962-63
Phillip H. De Lacy, Northwestern University, 1963-64
Norman T. Pratt, Indiana University, 1964-65
Henry C. Montgomery, Miami University, 1965-66
William H. Willis, Duke University, 1966-67
Francis L. Newton, Duke University, 1967-68
Roger A. Hornsby, University of Iowa, 1968-69
Paul L. MacKendrick, University of Wisconsin, 1969-70
Arthur F. Stocker, University of Virginia, 1970-71
Herbert W. Benario, Emory University, 1971-72
Alexander G. McKay, McMaster University, 1972-73
Paul R. Murphy, Ohio University, 1973-74
James W. Alexander, University of Georgia, 1974-75
Kenneth J. Reckford, University of North Carolina, 1975-76
Laura V. Sumner, Mary Washington College, 1976-77
Charles L. Babcock, Ohio State University, 1977-78
Lynette Thompson, Florida State University, 1978-79

Harry C. Rutledge, University of Tennessee, 1979-80
G. Karl Galinsky, University of Texas, 1980-81
Mark P. O. Morford, Ohio State University, 1981-82
Anna Lydia Motto, University of South Florida, 1982-83
Susan Ford Wiltshire, Vanderbilt University, 1983-84
Eleanor G. Huzar, Michigan State University, 1984-85
Gareth L. Schmeling, University of Florida, 1985-86
Theodore A. Tarkow, University of Missouri, 1986-87
Ernst A. Fredricksmeyer, University of Colorado, 1987-88
Ward W. Briggs, Jr., University of South Carolina, 1988-89

## FIRST VICE-PRESIDENTS
### OF THE
## CLASSICAL ASSOCIATION OF THE MIDDLE WEST AND SOUTH

Arthur T. Walker, University of Kansas, 1905-06
Frederick C. Eastman, Iowa State Normal School, 1906-07
Walter Dennison, University of Michigan, 1907-08
Ellsworth D. Wright, Lawrence University, 1908-09
Grove E. Barber, University of Nebraska, 1909-10
Charles W. Peppler, Emory College, 1910-11
Frederick W. Shipley, Washington University, 1911-12
Joseph E. Harry, University of Cincinnati, 1912-13
Daniel D. Haines, Wabash College, 1913-14
Harriet R. Kirby, North High School, Columbus, Ohio, 1914-15
Charles E. Little, Peabody College for Teachers, 1915-16
Frances E. Sabin, University of Wisconsin, 1916-17
Daniel A. Penick, University of Texas, 1917-18
Loura B. Woodruff, Oak Park, Illinois, High School, 1918-19
Gilbert C. Scoggin, University of Missouri, 1919-20
M. Julia Bentley, Hughes High School, Cincinnati, 1920-21
Mary Leal Harkness, Sophie Newcomb College, 1921-22
Emily H. Dutton, Tennessee College, 1922-23
T. Jennie Green, State Teachers College, Kirksville, Missouri, 1923-24
Elizabeth McGorey, Glenville High School, Cleveland, 1924-25
Mattie B. McLeod, South Texas Teachers College, 1925-26
Elizabeth M. Roff, Ashland High School, Kentucky, 1926-27
Dorothy M. Roehm, Northwestern High School, Detroit, 1927-28
Nellie Angel Smith, Western Tennessee State Teachers College, 1928-29
Calla A. Guyles, University of Wisconsin, 1929-30
Marie B. Denneen, North Carolina College for Women, 1930-31
Hubert McN. Poteat, Wake Forest College, 1931-32
Sally S. Lovelace, Jefferson High School, Roanoke, Virginia, 1932-33

Gertrude Smith, University of Chicago, 1933-34
Lena B. Tomson, Milwaukee-Downer College, Milwaukee, 1934-35
Sibyl Stonecipher, Western Kentucky Teachers College, 1935-36
Lucy Prichard, Marshall College, 1936-37
Mary V. Braginton, Rockford College, 1937-38
Franklin H. Potter, University of Iowa, 1938-39
Gladys Busch, Hughes High School, Cincinnati, 1939-40
H. J. Bassett, South Western College, Memphis, 1940-41
Eva May Newman, College of Wooster, 1941-42
Grace Beede, University of South Dakota, 1942-43
Irene Crabb, Evanston High School, Evanston, Illinois, 1943-44
A. P. Hamilton, University of Mississippi, 1944-45
Nellie Angel Smith, Memphis State College, Tennessee, 1945-46
Marie B. Denneen, Womens College of University of North Carolina,
    1946-47
Charlotte Ludlum, Berea College, 1947-48
Lillian R. Hadley, Steinmetz High School, Chicago, 1948-49
Graydon W. Regenos, Tulane University, 1949-50
Esther Weightman, Wisconsin High School, Madison, 1950-51
Grace Beede, University of South Dakota, 1951-52
H. G. Robertson, University of Toronto, 1952-53
Lucy Whitsel, Marshall College, 1953-54
Donnis Martin, Winthrop College, 1954-55
Demetrius J. Georgacas, University of North Dakota, 1955-56
Esther Weightman, Wisconsin High School, Madison, 1956-57
Graves H. Thompson, Hampden-Sydney College, 1957-58
Mary C. Arnold, Cambridge High School, Ohio, 1958-59
Sister M. Bede Donelan, College of St. Teresa, 1959-60
Ellen Machin, Central College, Missouri, 1960-61
Margaret M. Forbes, University of Minnesota, 1961-62
Joan M. Madsen, Oak Park and River Forest High School, Oak Park,
    Illinois, 1962-63
Ernestine F. Leon, University of Texas, 1963-64
Hazel E. Barnes, University of Colorado, 1964-65
Lois Ashton Larson, York Community High School, Elmhurst, Illinois,
    1965-66
Gertrude Ewing, Indiana State University, 1966-67
Margaret M. Forbes, University of Minnesota, 1967-68
Vivia Craig, Seacrest High School, Delray Beach, Florida, 1968-69
H. R. Butts, Birmingham-Southern University, 1969-70
Harry C. Rutledge, University of Tennessee, 1970-71
Mary A. Boxwell, Fort Dodge High School, Iowa, 1971-72

Lois T. Ellsworth, Bartlesville, Oklahoma, 1972-73
Lucile Cox Jones, Mary Washington College, 1973-74
Dorothy V. Daniel, Webster Groves High School, Missouri, 1974-75
Edith M. A. Kovach, University of Detroit, 1975-76
John D'Arms, University of Michigan, 1976-77
Theodore J. Tracy, S. J., University of Illinois at Chicago Circle, 1977-78
Ruth Froberg, Benjamin Franklin High School, Valparaiso, Indiana,
        1978-79
Louise Price Hoy, Marshall University, 1979-80
Raymond Den Adel, Rockford College, 1980-81
Laura Hughes, Northside High School, Atlanta, 1981-82
Dorothy V. Daniel, Kirkwood, Missouri, 1982-83
Robert M. Wilhelm, Miami University, 1983-84
George W. Houston, University of North Carolina, 1984-85
Elaine Fantham, University of Toronto, 1985-86
C. Wayne Tucker, Hampden-Sydney College, 1986-87
Maureen O'Donnell, North Springfield, Virginia, 1987-88
Karelisa V. Hartigan, University of Florida, 1988-89

## THE SECRETARY–TREASURERS
### OF THE
### CLASSICAL ASSOCIATION OF THE MIDDLE WEST AND SOUTH

Benjamin L. D'Ooge, Michigan State Normal College, 1905-08
Theodore C. Burgess, Bradley Polytechnic Institute, 1908-11
Herbert J. Barton, University of Illinois, 1911-15
Louis E. Lord, Oberlin College, 1915-20
Rollin H. Tanner, Denison University, 1920-23
Wilbert L. Carr, Oberlin College; later, University of Michigan, 1923-30
John O. Lofberg, Oberlin College, 1930-32
Fred S. Dunham, University of Michigan, 1932-42
Norman J. DeWitt, Washington University, 1942-45
William C. Korfmacher, St. Louis University, 1945-51
John N. Hough, University of Colorado, 1951-59
Paul R. Murphy, Ohio University, 1959-69
Galen O. Rowe, University of Pittsburgh and University of Iowa, 1969-71
Robert A. Tucker, University of Georgia, 1971-73
W. W. de Grummond, Florida State University, 1973-75
Gareth L. Schmeling, University of Florida, 1975-81
Roy E. Lindahl, Jr., Furman University, 1981-

## EXECUTIVE COMMITTEE

In addition to the President, First Vice-President, and Secretary-Treasurer the following have served as Members of the Executive Committee. Beginning in 1922 the immediate past president is recorded as serving one year *ex officio* on this Committee. Since 1954, the President-Elect has also served *ex officio*.

W. G. Hale, University of Chicago, 1905-19

G. E. Barber, University of Nebraska, 1905-09

F. W. Shipley, Washington University, 1906-10

Walter Hullihen, Grant University, 1907-08, 1913-17

B. L. D'Ooge, Michigan State Normal College, 1908-10, 1913-14

Walter Miller, University of Missouri, 1909-11

H. W. Johnston, University of Indiana, 1910-12

O. F. Long, Northwestern University, 1910-12, 1931-32

Robert B. Steele, Vanderbilt University, 1911-13, 1923-27

Josiah B. Game, Alabama State Normal College, 1912-16

Francis W. Kelsey, University of Michigan, 1914-17, 1917-18

A. L. Bondurant, University of Mississippi, 1916-20, 1925-26

J. B. Pike, University of Minnesota, 1917-21

Charles E. Little, George Peabody College, 1918-22, 1928-29

Charles H. Weller, University of Iowa, 1919-21, 1922-23

Daniel W. Lothman, East High School, Cleveland, 1920-23

Selatie E. Stout, University of Indiana, 1921-25, 1927-28

Alfred W. Milden, University of Mississippi, 1921-24

W. J. Battle, University of Texas, 1922-26, 1930-31

Arthur Keith, University of South Dakota, 1923-28

B. L. Ullman, University of Iowa, 1924-25

Roy C. Flickinger, University of Iowa, 1925-29, 1930-32, 1933-34

F. J. Miller, University of Chicago, 1926-27

J. O. Lofberg, Washington and Lee University; later, Oberlin College, 1926-30

A. M. Rovelstad, St. Olaf College; later, University of North Dakota, 1927-31

G. A. Harrer, University of North Carolina, 1928-32, 1934-36

R. J. Bonner, University of Chicago, 1929-30

H. J. Bassett, Southwestern, 1929-33

C. C. Mierow, Colorado College; later, Carleton College, 1931-35

Lillian Gay Berry, Indiana University, 1932-33

Rodney P. Robinson, University of Cincinnati, 1932-34

Eugene Tavenner, Washington University, 1932-36

A. Pelzer Wagener, College of William and Mary, 1933-37
Victor D. Hill, Ohio University, 1934-35
Edward K. Turner, Emory University, 1935-39
Norman W. DeWitt, University of Toronto, 1936-38
Alfred P. Dorjahn, Northwestern University, 1937-39
Emma B. Peters, Gary, Indiana, 1938-40
Marbury B. Ogle, University of Minnesota, 1938-42
L. R. Dean, Denison University, 1939-41
William E. Gwatkin, Jr., University of Missouri, 1939-41
Dorothy M. Bell, Oberlin College, 1940-41
Walter Agard, University of Wisconsin, 1941-44
Clyde Pharr, Vanderbilt University, 1941-43
Oscar W. Reinmuth, University of Texas, 1942-47
Preston H. Epps, University of North Carolina, 1943-44
Mars Westington, Hanover College, 1943-47
John L. Heller, University of Minnesota, 1944-48
Clyde Murley, Northwestern University, 1944-45
Fred S. Dunham, University of Michigan, 1945-49
Clarence A. Forbes, University of Nebraska; later, Ohio State University,
    1947-50
Arthur H. Moser, University of Tennessee, 1947-50
Gerald F. Else, University of Iowa, 1948-51
Henry C. Montgomery, Miami University, 1949-53
Wilbert L. Carr, University of Kentucky, 1950-54
Russel M. Geer, Tulane University, 1951-52
Ortha J. Wilner, State Teachers College, Milwaukee, 1952-55
James E. Dunlap, University of Michigan, 1952-56
H. Lloyd Stow, Vanderbilt University, 1953-57
Harry J. Leon, University of Texas, 1954-56
Robert J. Getty, University of Toronto; later, University of North Carolina,
    1955-59
Bert H. Narveson, St. Olaf College, 1956-60
Chauncey E. Finch, St. Louis University, 1956-68
Herman R. Butts, Birmingham-Southern College, 1957-61
Walter Allen, Jr., University of North Carolina, 1958-60
Paul L. MacKendrick, University of Wisconsin, 1959-63
William H. Willis, University of Mississippi, 1960-62
William M. Seaman, Michigan State University, 1960-64
Virgil E. Hiatt, Butler University, 1961-65
Arthur F. Stocker, University of Virginia, 1962-66
D. Herbert Abel, Loyola University, Chicago, 1963-67
Joseph M. Conant, Emory University, 1964-68

Richard T. Scanlan, University of Illinois, 1965-69
Edith M. A. Kovach, University of Detroit, 1966-70
Edwin L. Brown, University of North Carolina, 1967-71
James W. Alexander, University of Georgia, 1968-72
Donald R. Laing, Jr., Case Western Reserve University, 1969-73
Charles L. Babcock, Ohio State University, 1970-74
Laura V. Sumner, Mary Washington College, 1971-75
Silvio Skefich, Indiana University, 1972-74
Edward L. Bassett, University of Chicago, 1973-77
Edward Brooks, Jr., Macalester College, 1974-78
Glanville Downey, Indiana University, 1974-75
George Kennedy, University of North Carolina, 1975-79
William Fairchild, Michigan State University, 1975-76
Barbara H. Fowler, University of Wisconsin, 1976-80
Brent M. Froberg, University of South Dakota, 1977-81, 1987-
J. Ward Jones, College of William and Mary, 1978-82
Richard A. LaFleur, University of Georgia, 1979-83
Arthur G. Robson, Beloit College, 1980-84
James M. May, St. Olaf College, 1981-85
Sheila K. Dickison, University of Florida, 1982-86
Jane E. Phillips, University of Kentucky, 1983-87
Eleanor Winsor Leach, Indiana University, 1984-88
David F. Bright, University of Illinois, 1985-
James O. Loyd, Indiana State University, 1986-
James L. Franklin, Jr., Indiana University, 1988-

## EDITORS OF THE *CLASSICAL JOURNAL*
### EDITORS-IN-CHIEF*

Arthur Fairbanks, University of Iowa, 1905-07
Gordon J. Laing, University of Chicago, 1905-08
A. G. Laird, University of Wisconsin, 1907-09
Frank J. Miller, University of Chicago, 1908-28
Arthur T. Walker, University of Kansas, 1909-32
Roy C. Flickinger, University of Iowa, 1928-33
J. O. Lofberg, Oberlin College (died Nov. 10, 1932)
Walter Miller, University of Missouri, 1933-35
Eugene Tavenner, Washington University, 1935-45
Norman J. DeWitt, Washington University, 1945-50
Clyde Murley, Northwestern University, 1950-55
Phillip DeLacy, Washington University, 1955-56
Norman T. Pratt, Jr., Indiana University, 1956-61
W. Robert Jones, Ohio State University, 1961-68

Roy Arthur Swanson, University of Wisconsin-Milwaukee, 1968-73
Harold D. Evjen, University of Colorado, 1973-77
Ernst A. Fredricksmeyer, University of Colorado, Co-editor, 1973-76
Hunter R. Rawlings, III, University of Colorado, 1977-83
W. W. de Grummond, Florida State University, 1983-

> *Called Managing Editors from 1905 to 1922. The editorial office was at the University of Chicago from 1905 to 1925, at the University of Kansas from 1925 to 1928, and at the University of Iowa from 1928 to 1933, and at the institution of the Editor-in-Chief thereafter. From 1931-52 the Editor-in-Chief was also Business Manager.

## ASSOCIATE EDITORS

Abram Brown, East High School, Columbus, Ohio, 1905-07
A. G. Laird, University of Wisconsin, 1905-07
Walter Miller, Tulane University; later, University of Missouri, 1905-33
Henry A. Sanders, University of Michigan, 1905-06
J. J. Schlicher, Indiana State Normal School, 1905-15
Campbell Bonner, Peabody College for Teachers;
   later, University of Michigan, 1906-09
Charles D. Adams, Dartmouth College, 1907-08
W. J. Battle, University of Texas, 1907-08
Clarence W. Gleason, Volkman School,;
   later, Roxbury Latin School, Boston, 1907-39
Daniel W. Lothman, East High School, Cleveland, 1907-32
F. C. Eastman, University of Iowa, 1908-18
George H. Chase, Harvard University, 1908-28
John A. Scott, Northwestern University, 1909-33
Gilbert C. Scoggin, University of Missouri, 1915-25
Julianne A. Roller, Franklin High School, Portland, Oregon, 1915-27
Bertha Green, Hollywood High School, Los Angeles, 1916-21
George Howe, University of North Carolina, 1920-34
Berthold L. Ullman, University of Iowa, 1920-28
Walter A. Edwards, Los Angeles High School, 1921-29
Victor D. Hill, Ohio University, 1925-28, 1932-35
Marie B. Denneen, North Carolina College for Women, 1928-31
John Barker Stearns, Dartmouth College, 1929-37
W. A. Ellis, Lombard, Illinois, 1929-35
Arthur P. McKinlay, University of California, 1929-30
Frederic S. Dunn, University of Oregon, 1930-36
Frederick J. Lazell, University of Iowa, 1930-32
Calla A. Guyles, University of Wisconsin, 1931-32

Dorrance S. White, University of Iowa, 1930-33; 1949-52
Roy C. Flickinger, University of Iowa, 1933-41
Dorothy M. Bell, Oberlin College, 1933-40
Eugene Tavenner, Washington University, 1933-35
Franklin H. Potter, University of Iowa, 1933-53
Fred L. Farley, College of the Pacific, 1934-44
G. A. Harrer, University of North Carolina, 1934-43
Alfred P. Dorjahn, Northwestern University, 1935-43
Dwight N. Robinson, Ohio Wesleyan University, 1935-41
Adolph F. Pauli, Wesleyan University, 1937-46
John W. Spaeth, Jr., Wesleyan University, 1937-49
Russel M. Geer, Tulane University, 1937-46
George E. Lane, Thayer Academy, Braintree, Massachusetts, 1939-53
Grace L. Beede, University of South Dakota, 1940-52
Kevin Guinagh, Eastern Illinois State Teachers College, 1941-46
John N. Hough, Ohio State University, 1941-46
John L. Heller, University of Minnesota, 1943-50
A. E. Gordon, University of California, 1944-47
W. M. Green, University of California, 1947-53
Van L. Johnson, Tufts College, 1947-49
Edward L. Bassett, Cornell University, 1947-49
Lionel Casson, New York University, 1947-49
George Yanitelli, New York University, 1947-49
Stuart Crawford, Boston University, 1949-53
Eugene Miller, University of Pittsburgh, 1949-53

## ASSISTANT EDITORS

Thomas S. Duncan, Washington University, 1935-45
Oscar E. Nybakken, University of Iowa, 1945-46
William C. Salyer, Washington University, 1947-50
Grundy Steiner, Northwestern University, 1950-53

## EDITORS FOR NEW ENGLAND

Charles D. Adams, Dartmouth College, 1908-13
Monroe N. Wetmore, Williams College, 1913-20
sidney N. Deane, Smith College, 1920-24
Joseph W. Hewitt, Wesleyan University, 1924-27
Harry M. Hubbell, Yale University, 1927-30
Russel M. Geer, Brown University, 1930-37
Herbert N. Couch, Brown University, 1937-41, 1942-46
Frank Pierce Jones, Brown University, 1941-42

James A. Notopoulos, Trinity College, 1946-67
Katherine Geffcken, Wellesley College, 1967-69, 1970-77
Barbara McCarthy, Wellesley College, 1969-70
Mary R. Lefkowitz, Wellesley College, 1977-83
William C. Scott, Dartmouth College, 1983-

## EDITORS FOR THE PACIFIC STATES

Herbert C. Nutting, University of California, 1916-30
Arthur P. McKinlay, U.C.L.A., 1930-51
W. M. Green, University of California, 1951-62
William S. Anderson, University of California, 1962-67
W. R. Johnson, University of California, 1967-74

## EDITOR FOR THE PACIFIC NORTHWEST

Anthony J. Podlecki, University of British Columbia, 1977-

## EDITOR FOR THE MIDDLE WESTERN STATES

William E. Gwatkin, University of Missouri, 1933-35

## EDITORS FOR THE ATLANTIC STATES

Franklin B. Krauss, Pennsylvania State University, 1945-66
J. Hilton Turner, Westminster College (PA), 1966-74
Diskin W. Clay, Haverford College and The Johns Hopkins University, 1974-78
John Van Sickle, Brooklyn College and CUNY, 1978-82
Harry B. Evans, Fordham University, 1982-85
Robert J. Penella, Fordham University, 1985-

## BOOK REVIEW EDITORS

William S. Salyer, Washington University, 1949-50
Grundy Steiner, Northwestern University, 1950-56
Fred W. Householder, Indiana University, 1956-58, 1959-61
Verne B. Schuman, Indiana University, 1958-59
Robert J. Lenardon, Ohio State University, 1961-68
H. James Shey, University of Wisconsin-Milwaukee, 1968-73
Hunter R. Rawlings, III, University of Colorado, 1973-77
Harold D. Evjen, University of Colorado, 1977-83
E. Christian Kopff, University of Colorado, 1977-87
Sheila K. Dickison, University of Florida, 1987-

# Appendix II

## VICE-PRESIDENTS FOR THE STATES AND PROVINCES

ALABAMA
W. B. Saffold, University P. O., 1905-1909
Malcolm C. Burke, University P. O., 1909
Edward L. Colebeck, Birmingham, 1909-11
David M. Key, Greensboro, 1911-13
Allen J. Moon, Birmingham, 1913-17
Hortense Thornton, Birmingham, 1917-24
George Currie, Birmingham, 1924-28
Harriet Dale Johnson, Marion, 1928-32
Cora E. Kercher, Montgomery, 1932-35
Clara Belle Senn, Birmingham, 1935-40
Edgar C. Reinke, Montevallo, 1940-43
David M. Key, Birmingham, 1943-45
Ledia Kate Poyner, Montgomery, 1945-46
Gordon L. Keyes, Birmingham, 1946-47
Sister M. Ann Patrick Ware, Mobile, 1947-49
H. R. Butts, Birmingham, 1949-57
Charles D. Perry, University, 1957-78
Elisabeth McNair, Tuscaloosa, 1978-81
Nancy Worley, Decatur and New Hope, 1981-

ARKANSAS
J. C. Futrall, Fayetteville, 1905-08, 1910-13
Cheever Hoyt, Little Rock, 1908-10
Guy A. Simmons, Conway, 1913-24
H. H. Strauss, Fayetteville, 1924-26
H. W. Camp, Conway, 1926-39
Essie Hill, Little Rock, 1939-46
Ruth Boggs, Fayetteville, 1946-49
Bertie Johnston, Little Rock, 1949-55
Chester Neudling, Fayetteville, 1955-58
Mary L. H. Henbest, Fayetteville, 1958-60
Robert B. Cross, Fayetteville, 1960-80
Daniel B. Levine, Fayetteville, 1980-86
Joan Carr, Fayetteville, 1986-

## COLORADO
Virginia Beauchamp, Colorado Springs, 1905-09
Ralph S. Pitts, Denver, 1909-10, 1915-17
Milo G. Derham, Boulder, 1910-12, 1935-37
Samuel S. Kingsbury, Boulder, 1912-13
Annette Badgley, Denver, 1913-15
Hiram Gillespie, Westminster, 1917
Charles C. Mierow, Colorado Springs, 1917-24
E. D. Cressman, Denver, 1924-31
Myra C. Langley, Denver, 1931-35
Karl K. Hulley, Boulder, 1937-40, 1944-66
Maynard A. Iungerich, Colorado Springs, 1940-43
Edna Dessaint, Colorado Springs, 1943-44
Harold D. Evjen, Boulder, 1966-72
Joy K. King, Boulder, 1972-82
Tamara Bauer, Denver, 1982-

## FLORIDA
B. C. Bondurant, Tallahassee, 1908-09
Frances N. Clayton, Tampa, 1909-11
Clarence E. Boyd, Tallahassee, 1911-13
James N. Anderson, Gainesville, 1913-16
Josiah B. Game, Tallahassee, 1916-35
Olivia Dorman, Tallahassee, 1935-42
Gladys Laird, Gainesville, 1942-54
Vivia Craig, Jacksonville, 1954-78
Geraldine Hodges, Gainesville, 1978-82
Elizabeth Hunter, Jacksonville, 1982-87
Marcia Stille, Lakeland, 1987-

## GEORGIA
C. W. Peppler, Oxford, 1908-12
William D. Hooper, Athens, 1912-17
E. K. Turner, Oxford, 1917-24
Clarence Boyd, Atlanta, 1924-31
Evelyn B. Ewing, Atlanta, 1931-40
Katherine Torrance, Decatur, 1940-42
Annabelle Horn, Macon, 1942-44
Susan P. Cobbs, Decatur, 1944-45
M. Kathryn Glick, Decatur, 1945-61
Joseph M. Conant, Atlanta, 1961-68
Herbert W. Benario, Atlanta, 1968-70

Dorothy Cavan, Thomaston, 1970-76
Lillie B. Hamilton, College Park, 1976-87
Elizabeth Frank, Atlanta, 1987-

IDAHO
Harold L. Axtell, Moscow, 1908-11
Herbert D. Cheney, Pocatello, 1911-16
Florence Sharp, Twin Falls, 1916

ILLINOIS
Theodore C. Burgess, Peoria, 1905-1908
H. J. Barton, Champaign, 1908-11
William T. McCoy, Chicago, 1911
William F. Beardsley, Evanston, 1911-13
Omera F. Long, Evanston, 1913-14
Ellen A. Ford, Charleston, 1914-16
Harriet Bouldin, Springfield, 1916-17
Rollin H. Tanner, Jacksonville, 1917
Loura Woodruff, Oak Park, 1917-19
Keith Preston, Evanston, 1919-21
Clyde Murley, Evanston, 1921-28
Dorothea Nevius, Evanston, 1928-29
Florence Brubaker, Oak Park, 1929-37
Harriet Ecternach, Sterling, 1937-42
Kevin J. Guinagh, Charleston, 1942-43
Norman B. Johnson, Galesburg, 1943-46
Charles J. Adamec, Galesburg, 1946-48
Lillian R. Hadley, Chicago, 1948-51
Ellen Machin, Alton, 1951-58
Mary Jeannette Munce, Bloomington, 1958-75
Raymond Den Adel, Rockford, 1975-78
Naidyne Bridwell, Barrington, 1978-85
Vacant 1985-86
Donald Hoffman, Chicago, 1986-

INDIANA
Lillian G. Berry, Bloomington, 1905-08, 1921-32
Daniel D. Hains, Crawfordsville, 1908-13, 1915-17
Anna F. Weaver, Indianapolis, 1913-15
Frank H. Cowles, Crawfordsville, 1917-19
Ella G. Marthens, Indianapolis, 1919
H. C. Merrill, Franklin, 1919-20

Selatie E. Stout, Bloomington, 1920-21
R. H. Coon, Bloomington, 1932-35
Dade B. Shearer, Greencastle, 1935-39
Verne B. Schuman, Bloomington, 1939-49
Anne Dale Kek, Indianapolis, 1949-55
Virgil Hiatt, Indianapolis, 1955-65
Gertrude Ewing, Terre Haute, 1965-75
James Loyd, Terre Haute, 1975-81
Albert Steiner, Indianapolis, 1981-88
Bernard F. Barcio, Indianapolis, 1988-

IOWA
F. C. Eastman, Iowa City, 1905-09, 1917-18
Charles N. Smiley, Grinnell, 1909-17
Franklin H. Potter, Iowa City, 1919-23
J. M. Brigham, Mt. Vernon; later, Grinnell, 1923-31
Margaret A. Pratt, Fort Dodge, 1931-33
Minnie Keys Flickinger, Iowa City, 1933-35
Mark E. Hutchinson, Mt. Vernon, 1935-39
H. R. Butts, Iowa City, 1939-42
Marguerite Struble, Cedar Falls, 1942-44
Oscar E. Nybakken, Iowa City, 1944-55
Mary Boxwell, Ft. Dodge, 1955-72
Charles Milhauser, Mount Vernon, 1972-75
Archie Bush, Iowa City, 1975-80
Gerald Lalonde, Grinnell, 1980-86
Jeffrey L. Buller, Dubuque, 1986-

KANSAS
A. T. Walker, Lawrence, 1905-08
Ralph L. Ward, Kansas City, 1908-09
Warren S. Gordis, Ottawa, 1909-12
Irene Nye, Topeka, 1912-15
Homer K. Ebright, Baldwin City, 1915-16
O. G. Markham, Baldwin, 1916-24
W. L. Holtz, Emporia, 1924-40
Mary A. Grant, Lawrence, 1940-46
Winnie Lowrance, Lawrence, 1946-49, 1954-55
Maude Beamer, Lawrence, 1949-50
L. R. Lind, Lawrence, 1950-54, 1955-62
Frances McKenna, Tecumseh, 1962-67
Oliver C. Phillips, Lawrence, 1967-72, 1980-

Alma Rowlands, Emporia, 1972-80

KENTUCKY
Florence P. Witherspoon, Louisville, 1905-08
Glanville Terrell, Georgetown, 1908-10
Thomas B. Macartney, Lexington, 1910-12
Theodore T. Jones, Lexington, 1912-15
Thomas T. Jones, Lexington, 1915-16
M. A. Leiper, Bowling Green, 1916-20
George Ragland, Georgetown, 1920-23
Elizabeth M. Roff, Ashland, 1923-31
Mabel H. Pollitt, Richmond, 1931-32
F. C. Grise, Bowling Green, 1932-40
Charlotte Ludlum, Berea, 1940-50
J. W. D. Skiles, Lexington, 1950-56
Robert J. Buck, Lexington, 1956-60
Mrs. Howard Whitehead, Lexington, 1960-61
Thomas H. Corcoran, Lexington, 1961-62
Alexander M. Gilchrist, Lexington, 1962-67
Lawrence S. Thompson, Lexington, 1967-70
Hubert Martin, Jr., Lexington, 1970-75
Jane E. Phillips, Lexington, 1975-81
Robert Rabel, Lexington, 1981-84
Mary Beth Hoffman, Danville, 1984-87
J. Drew Harrington, Bowling Green, 1987-

LOUISIANA
J. H. Dillard, New Orleans, 1905-08
Walter Miller, New Orleans, 1908-09
Edward A. Bechtel, New Orleans, 1909-11, 1917-19, 1921-22
Mary L. Harkness, New Orleans, 1911-17, 1919-21
Myra Rogers, New Orleans, 1922-26, 1929-32
Ernest Riedel, New Orleans, 1926-29
Susan Dinsmore Tew, New Orleans, 1932-34
Mary C. Stevens, New Orleans, 1934-40
Graydon W. Regenos, New Orleans, 1940-58
Thomas H. Corcoran, Baton Rouge, 1958-59
Russel M. Geer, New Orleans, 1959-61
Richard M. Frazer, Jr., New Orleans, 1961-66
Sanford G. Etheridge, New Orleans, 1966-80
Kenneth F. Kitchell, Jr., Baton Rouge, 1980-82
Charlayne Allan, Baton Rouge, 1982-85, 1988-
Lora H. Kehoe, New Orleans, 1985-88

## MANITOBA
Edmund G. Berry, Winnipeg, 1971-80
Rory B. Egan, Winnipeg, 1980-

## MICHIGAN
Walter Dennison, Ann Arbor, 1905-08, 1909-10
A. R. Crittenden, Olivet, 1908-09
G. R. Swain, Bay City, 1910-11
J. Remsen Bishop, Detroit, 1911-14
Cheever Hoyt, Detroit, 1914-20
Clara J. Allison, Ypsilanti, 1920-21, 1928-34
Laura N. Wilson, Grand Rapids, 1921-22
F. O. Bates, Detroit, 1922
Dorothy Roehm, Detroit, 1922-27
Anna M. Barnard, Mt. Pleasant, 1927-28
M. Berry Wood, Muskegon, 1934-36
Eunice Kraft, Kalamazoo, 1936-38
Irma Anschutz, Bay City, 1938-42
Elizabeth B. Lawry, Lansing, 1942-43
Helen Wilson, Dearborn, 1943-44
Ruth Hetzman, Royal Oak, 1944-49
Emile J. Stern, Detroit, 1949-55
William M. Seaman, East Lansing, 1955-60
Edith M. A. Kovach, Detroit, 1960-76
William Fairchild, East Lansing, 1976-80
Elizabeth Giedeman, Kalamazoo, 1980-83
William S. Thomson, Olivet, 1983-88
Mary Yelda, Detroit, 1987-

## MINNESOTA
J. E. Granrud, Minneapolis, 1905-09
Joseph B. Pike, Minneapolis, 1909-13
Esther Friedlander, Minneapolis, 1913-17
Arthur L. Keith, Northfield, 1917-21
Dorrance S. White, Minneapolis, 1921-23
H. Osborne Ryder, St. Paul, 1923-25
Marie Denneen, Minneapolis, 1925-26
Mary C. Harris, Minneapolis, 1926-31
Eleanor P. Marlowe, Minneapolis, 1931-39
John L. Heller, Minneapolis, 1939-44
Hays P. Archerd, St. Paul, 1944-48
B. H. Narveson, Northfield, 1948-57

Sister M. Bede Donelan, Winona, 1957-68
Alvin P. Traaseth, Hopkins, 1968-70
Ronald Replogle, Hopkins, 1970-73
Jeremiah Reedy, St. Paul, 1973-75
Helen Moritz, Minneapolis, 1975-78
William Freiert, St. Peter, 1978-85
Stanley Iverson, Moorhead, 1985-

MISSISSIPPI
J. L. Deupree, University P.O., 1905-08
M. W. Swartz, Jackson, 1908-10
A. J. Aven, Clinton, 1910-12
Alfred W. Milden, University, 1912-14, 1917-24
J. Beverly F. Shaw, Meridian, 1914-17
Lucy Hutchins, Blue Mountain, 1924-28
A. P. Hamilton, Jackson, 1928-31, 1940-64
Clara W. Stokes, Jackson, 1931-34
Gladys Martin, Columbus, 1934-40
Evelyn Lee Way, University, 1964-72
Edward Capps, III, University, 1972-78
Eleanor Wimmett, University, 1978-80
James Barfield, Jackson, 1980-82
Catherine Freis, Jackson, 1982-86
Robert Babcock, Mississippi State, 1986-87
Mark Clark, Hattiesburg, 1987-

MISSOURI
W. G. Manly, Columbia, 1906-11
Frederick W. Shipley, St. Louis, 1911-12
Walter Miller, Columbia, 1912-13
Howard G. Colwell, St. Louis, 1913-15
Arthur P. Hall, Springfield, 1915-17
H. H. Armstrong, Springfield, 1917-18
F. C. Shaw, Kansas City, 1918-20
R. H. Coon, Liberty, 1920-23
Eugene Tavenner, St. Louis, 1923-30, 1932-35
F. M. Debatin, St. Louis, 1930-32
William C. Korfmacher, St. Louis, 1936-45
Ruth F. Joedicke, Clayton, 1945-54
Robert B. Hoerber, Fulton, 1955-65
Isabelle Schwerdtmann, Kirkwood, 1965-70
Claire Johnson, Saint Ann, 1970-72

Dorothy V. Daniel, Webster Groves, 1972-82
Luciana Csaki, Kansas City, 1982-84
Peter Viscusi, Warrensburg, 1984-86
Kathy Elifrits, Rolla, 1986-

NEBRASKA
Bessie J. Snyder, Omaha, 1905-09
Grove E. Barber, Lincoln, 1909-12
Olivia M. Pound, Lincoln, 1912-18
Susan Paxson, Omaha, 1918-21
Esther Clark, Peru, 1921-22
Ellen Rooney, Omaha, 1922-28
Jessie B. Jury, Lincoln, 1928-35
Alice Robinson, Kearney, 1935-38
H. R. Butts, Kearney, 1938-39
Bessie S. Rathbun, Omaha, 1939-43
Beulah Rundle, Wayne, 1943-44
Gertrude McEachen, Lincoln, 1944-53
Ruth Forbes, Omaha, 1953-54
Ruth Pilling, Omaha, 1954-75
Thomas N. Winter, Lincoln, 1975-80
Kathryn A. Thomas, Omaha, 1980-86
Rita Ryan, Omaha, 1986-

NEW MEXICO
C. B. Newcomer, State College, 1916-17
Lynn B. Mitchell, Albuquerque, 1917-19, 1928-38
Jeanette M. Inches, Albuquerque, 1919-28
Madalene Hendricks, Albuquerque, 1938-55
Anne Kingsbury, Albuquerque, 1955-56
Vacant 1956-57
Anne K. LeCroy, Albuquerque, 1957-60
Helen B. Carl, Alamogordo, 1960-67
Mary I. Steele, Albuquerque, 1967-70
Helen Merkle, Roswell, 1970-75
Warren S. Smith, Jr., Albuquerque, 1975-78
Nancy Lawrence, Albuquerque, 1978-83
Vacant 1983-84
Diana Robin, Albuquerque, 1984-87, 1988-
Geoffrey Harrison, Albuquerque, 1987-88

## NORTH CAROLINA
George W. Paschal, Wake Forest, 1908-09
George Howe, Chapel Hill, 1909-12, 1915-17
Thomas J. Wilson, Chapel Hill, 1912-14
Esther Snoddy, Red Springs, 1914-15
Charles W. Peppler, Durham, 1917
Helen H. Law, Raleigh, 1917-18, 1921-27
Hubert M. Poteat, Wake Forest, 1918-21
Marie B. Denneen, Greensboro, 1927-56
Charles Henderson, Jr., Chapel Hill, 1956-63
James N. Settle, Durham, 1963-66
Philip A. Stadter, Chapel Hill, 1966-67, 1968-72
Edwin L. Brown, Chapel Hill, 1967-68
William S. Thurman, Asheville, 1972-75
Guy Cooper, Asheville, 1975-80
Christina Elliott Sorum, Raleigh, 1980-82
Jeffrey Soles, Greensboro, 1982-
Mary Ellen Soles, Greensboro, 1982-

## NORTH DAKOTA
S. J. Pease, University P.O., 1905-08
Frederick E. Stratton, Fargo, 1908-11
May Bestor, Fargo, 1911
Guy R. Vowles, Fargo, 1911-22
Edgar A. Menk, Grand Forks, 1922-24, 1925-29
William W. Lloyd, Jamestown, 1924-25
Lillian Gubelman, Valley City, 1929-32
A. M. Rovelstad, Grand Forks, 1932-54
Demetrius J. Georgacas, Grand Forks, 1954-64
Louis Palanca, Grand Forks, 1964-67, 1968-80, 1982-?
James L. Elliott, Grand Forks, 1967-68
Laureen Beaver, Bismarck, 1980-82
Carol Andreini, Fargo, ?

## OHIO
S. C. Derby, Columbus, 1905-08
J. E. Harry, Cincinnati, 1908-10
W. G. Leutner, Cleveland, 1910-12
Harriet R. Kirby, Columbus, 1912-14
Elizabeth McGorey, Cleveland, 1914-15
Edwin L. Findley, Cleveland, 1915-23
Victor D. Hill, Athens, 1923-27

Elizabeth J. Adams, Columbus, 1927-28
M. Julia Bentley, Cincinnati, 1928-32
Dwight N. Robinson, Delaware, 1932-40
Anna H. Blake, Cleveland, 1940-44
Henry C. Montgomery, Oxford, 1944-48
Harlan R. Parker, Hudson, 1948-51
Adele Knight, Willoughby, 1951-55
Mary C. Arnold, Cambridge, 1955-76
Helen Glesen, Cincinnati, 1976-80
Judith Bluestein, Cincinnati, 1980-81
Robert M. Wilhelm, Oxford, 1981-85
Cynthia King, Dayton, 1985-

## OKLAHOMA
J. L. Imel, Edmond, 1905-08
Joseph F. Paxton, Norman, 1908-12
James W. Sturgis, Norman, 1912-17
Otto W. Jeffries, Edmond, 1917-30
Mary R. Bell, Chickasha, 1930-31, 1944-57
Isabel Work, Durant, 1931-40
Jessie Newby, Edmond, 1940-44
William R. Tongue, Norman, 1957-60
Philip J. Nolan, Norman, 1960-80
John S. Catlin, Norman, 1980-

## ONTARIO
John S. Bennett, Toronto, 1924-36
Harold Bennett, Toronto, 1936-38
David Breslove, Toronto, 1938-46
H. G. Robertson, Toronto, 1946-53
Emily McInnes, Cornwall, 1953-68
Alexander G. McKay, Hamilton, 1968-81
Ross S. Kilpatrick, Kingston, 1981-

## SASKATCHEWAN
Anabel Robinson, Regina, 1986-

## SOUTH CAROLINA
C. W. Peppler, Oxford, Ga., 1908-09
Robert P. Pell, Spartanburg, 1909-10
Edwin L. Green, Columbia, 1910-14, 1922-26
Mary Wilson Gee, Spartanburg, 1914-22

Donnis Martin, Rock Hill, 1926-31, 1949-58
Ruth Carroll, Hartsville & Newberry, 1931-44
Harold W. Miller, Greenville, 1944-49
Mary Frances Parker, Walterboro, 1958-72
Roy E. Lindahl, Jr., Greenville, 1972-81
Frank Morris, Charleston, 1981-85
Anne Leen, Greenville, 1985-

SOUTH DAKOTA
J. H. Howard, Vermillion, 1905-14, 1917-20
Louise French, Huron, 1914-17
Dorothy Printup, Britton, 1920-22
M. Catharine Brown, Watertown, 1922-23
Frank Olson, Aberdeen, 1923-26
Arthur L. Keith, Vermillion, 1926-29
Grace L. Beede, Vermillion, 1929-70
Brent M. Froberg, Vermillion, 1970-

TENNESSEE
B. L. Wiggins, Sewanee, 1905-08
Walter Hullihen, Chattanooga, 1908-12
Charles E. Little, Nashville, 1912-13
William R. Webb, Bell Buckle, 1913-14
David R. Lee, Chattanooga, 1914-25
R. B. Steele, Nashville, 1925-31
Nellie Angel Smith, Memphis, 1931-49
Isabelle Moser, Knoxville, 1949-54
Francis L. Newton, Nashville, 1954-67
John W. Zarker, Nashville, 1967-71
F. Carter Philips, Jr., Nashville, 1971-80
Harry C. Rutledge, Knoxville, 1980-

TEXAS
W. J. Battle, Austin, 1905-09
J. B. Eskridge, N. Waco, 1909-11
Mamie Brightwell, Fort Worth, 1911-15
Daniel A. Penick, Austin, 1915-22
Ruby Terrill, Commerce, 1922-23
J. N. Brown, Denton, 1923-31
Marion C. Butler, Waco, 1931-42
Harry J. Leon, Austin, 1942-50, 1952-56
J. D. Sadler, Lubbock, 1950-52

George F. Osmun, Austin, 1956-58
James A. Hitt, Austin, 1958-80
Edward George, Lubbock, 1980-86
James F. Johnson, Sherman, 1986-

UTAH
Frank H. Fowler, Salt Lake City, 1913-15
Alice E. Rowe, Salt Lake City, 1915-19
A. R. Anderson, Salt Lake City, 1919-23, 1925-28
Raymond Harriman, Salt Lake City, 1923-25
Marion Van Pelt, Salt Lake City, 1928-36, 1949-54
Mignonette Spilman, Salt Lake City, 1936-49
Mary Caffey, Salt Lake City, 1954-58
Vera D. Groshell, Salt Lake City, 1958-61
Joyce Warburton, Salt Lake City, 1961-63
Gerald K. Gresseth, Salt Lake City, 1963-72
William H. Hess, Salt Lake City, 1972-80
R. Douglas Philips, Provo, 1980-83
John F. Hall, Provo, 1983-

VIRGINIA
Charles E. Bishop, Williamsburg, 1908-09
Thomas Fitz Hugh, Charlottesville, 1909-10
J. W. Kern, Lexington, 1910-12
William H. Whiting, Jr., Hampden-Sydney, 1912-14
Herbert C. Lipscomb, Lynchburg, 1914-24
A. P. Wagener, Salem, 1924-26
J. O. Lofberg, Lexington, 1926-27
Sallie S. Lovelace, Roanoke, 1927-33
Susan Roberts, East Radford, 1933-37
George J. Ryan, Williamsburg, 1937-41
Graves H. Thompson, Hampden-Sydney, 1941-44
Gertrude Malz, Sweet Briar, 1944-63
Lucile Cox, Lynchburg, 1963-69
Lucile Cox Jones, Fredericksburg, 1969-76
Elizabeth Jones, Newport News, 1976-80
Linda Sharrard Montross, Vienna, 1980-84
John Oakley, Williamsburg, 1984-86, 1987-88
Martha G. Abbott, Annandale, 1986-87, 1988-

## WEST VIRGINIA

R. W. Douthat, Morgantown, 1905-08
Willa H. Butcher, Fairmount, 1908-09
F. M. Longanecker, Charleston, 1909-11
Harriet D. Johnson, Huntington, 1911-14
Charles Bishop, Morgantown, 1914-24
Lucy E. Prichard, Huntington, 1924-36
Helen DeBerry, Clarksburg, 1936-39
Grace Albright, Clarksburg, 1939-49
Lucy Whitsel, Huntington, 1949-63
Louise Price Hoy, Huntington, 1963-85
Charles O. Lloyd, Huntington, 1985-

## WISCONSIN

E. D. Wright, Appleton, 1905-08, 1910-11
Charlotte Wood, Whitewater, 1908-10
Wallace Riess, Milwaukee, 1911-13
Leta M. Wilson, Madison, 1913-14, 1922-23
Joseph G. Brandt, Madison, 1914-15
Frances E. Sabin, Madison, 1915-17
Lucia Spooner, Superior, 1917-18
Harriet Kuhns, Madison, 1918-19
J. N. Daland, Milton, 1919-22
Calla Guyles, Madison, 1923-31
Lena B. Tomson, Milwaukee, 1931-34
Esther Weightman, Madison, 1934-61
Shirley Jane Kaub, Madison, 1961-81
Arlene Silness, Janesville, 1981-83
James Greenwald, Milwaukee, 1983-87
William W. Kean, Suring, 1987-

## WYOMING

J. F. Soule, Laramie, 1916-17
Ida B. Hull, Sheridan, 1917-28
Maurine Hallo, Laramie, 1928-31
Rudy McBride, Casper, 1931-60
Ruth W. Bauder, Cheyenne, 1960-70
David R. Cunningham, Laramie, 1970-75
Constance Campbell, Cheyenne, 1975-80
Anna Maria Williams, Warren AFB, 1980-81
Vacant 1981-82
William Callahan, Casper, 1982-86
Mark S. Mathern, Casper, 1986-

# Appendix III

SEMPLE, GRANT, AND CAMWS SCHOLARSHIP WINNERS

1947 Cordelia Alderson, Humphrey, Nebraska; Rome
1948 Edith M. A. Kovach, Detroit, Michigan; Rome
1949 Lucile Cox, Lynchburg, Virginia; Rome
1950 Elizabeth Conn, Corinth, Mississippi; Athens
1951 Lois Robinson, Maywood, Illinois; Rome
1952 no award
1953 Mrs. J. H. Johnson, Kingsport, Tennessee; ?
1954 Elizabeth H. Ferguson, Grosse Pointe, Michigan; Athens
1955 Ruth D. Schroth, Kenosha, Wisconsin; Rome
1956 Mary Caffey, Salt Lake City, Utah; ?
1957 Richard R. Mickley, Louisville, Ohio; Rome
1958 Garth Lambert, Toronto, Ontario; Athens
1959 Margaret Mildred Welch, Oak Park, Illinois; Rome
1960 Geraldine Gesell, Oklahoma City, Oklahoma; Athens
     Mary Jane McNally, Chicago, Illinois; Athens
1961 Marie E. Young, Red Oak, Iowa; Rome
1962 Ruth Holl, New Knoxville, Ohio; Athens
1963 John Philip Dolan, Des Moines, Iowa; Rome
1964 Nancy Lou Lister, Cleveland, Ohio; Athens
1965 Kathleen M. Anglese, Barrington, Illinois; Rome
     Marion Leathers Daniels, Atlanta, Georgia; Athens
     Ann Elizabeth Werner, Fremont, Michigan; Cumae
1966 Helen Bair Biery, Kansas City, Missouri; Athens
     Frederic Fortney, Lake Forest, Illinois; Cumae
     Elizabeth Ronan, Menomonee Falls, Wisconsin; Rome
1967 Robert Stephen Baxter, S.J., New Orleans, Louisiana; Athens
     Sister M. Cynthia Klas, St. Nazianz, Wisconsin; Cumae
     Sister M. Ethel Wiedling, I.H.M., Dearborn, Michigan; Rome
1968 Rev. Loras C. Otting, Cedar Rapids, Iowa; Athens
     Kathryn D. DePue, Grand Ledge, Michigan; Cumae
     John E. Emmett, Cincinnati, Ohio; Rome
1969 Lynne Jones, Crestline, Ohio; Cumae
     Sister Marjorie McFarland, Detroit, Michigan; Rome
     Frederick J. Benda, S.J., Cuyahoga Falls, Ohio; Athens
1970 Naidyne B. Bridwell, Arlington Heights, Illinois; Athens
     Judith A. Bluestein, Bellefontaine, Ohio; Cumae
     Sister Frances, O.S.H., St. Andrews, Tennessee; Rome

1971   Carol Ann Cheff, Chicago, Illinois; Rome
       Geraldine Garant Hodges, Gainesville, Florida; Cumae
1972   Donald H. Hoffman, Chicago, Illinois; Athens
       Sister Edward Cecilia Schniedermeier, ?; Rome
1973   Sister Mary Isaac Jogues, Milwaukee, Wisconsin; Rome
       Sister Florence Gerdes, C.S.J., LaGrange Park, Illinois; Athens
1974   Ruth Godfrey, Key West, Florida; Rome
       Jane Woodruff, Vermillion, South Dakota; Athens
1975   Sister Florence Marie Richie, Elmhurst, Illinois; Rome
       Paul Vincent Denning, Jr., Fargo, North Dakota; Athens
1976   Susan Hall, Salem, Virginia; Rome
       Nellie Schmidt, Savannah, Georgia; Athens
1977   Donald Jacques, Chicago, Illinois; Rome
       Sharon Jensen, Sioux Falls, South Dakota; Athens
1978   Constance Campbell, Cheyenne, Wyoming; Rome
       Lynn Napiorski, Dallas, Texas; Athens
1979   Austin Gomez, University City, Missouri; Rome
       Bobbie Wrenn Root, Atlanta, Georgia; Athens
1980   Elizabeth Dobson, South Charleston, West Virginia; Rome
       Charlotte Goss, Knoxville, Tennessee; Athens
1981   Tamara J. Bauer, Boulder, Colorado; Rome
       Debra S. Burden, Martinsville, Indiana; Vergilian Society
       Josephine D. Jardine, Lubbock, Texas; Athens
       Cynthia Klas, Franklin, Wisconsin; Vergilian Society
       Norma T. Quarles, San Antonio, Texas; Athens
1982   Ede J. Ashworth, Wellsburg, West Virginia; Athens
       Sally Blair, Arlington, Virginia; Vergilian Society
       Louise B. Cobb, Charlotte, North Carolina; Vergilian Society
       Vincent O. Drago, Jackson, Mississippi; Rome
       Carter Stubbs Drake, Lexington, Virginia; Rome
1983   G. Edward Gaffney, Nashville, Tennessee; Athens
       Carol Ann Houston, Ann Arbor, Michigan; Rome
1984   Benjamin Lupica, Nount Vernon, Ohio; Athens
       Kathryn van der Pol, Houston, Texas; Rome
1985   Alan Blessing, St. Petersburg, Florida; Athens
       Dennis DeYoung, Savannah, Georgia; Rome
       Gerald A. Meyer, Saginaw, Michigan; Rome
1986   Cathy P. Daugherty, Ashland, Virginia; Athens
       Harry L. Perkins, Richmond, Virginia; Rome
       Patsy Ricks, Jackson, Mississippi; Vergilian Society

1987   Deena Berg, Austin, Texas; Rome
       Joseph Ewbank, Atlanta, Georgia; Rome
       Barbara Felkel, Kalamazoo, Michigan; Rome
       Edith Keene, Durham, North Carolina; Rome
1988   John Breuker, Jr., Hudson, Ohio; Vergilian Society
       Donald H. Hoffman, Chicago, Illinois; Vergilian Society
       Cathy E. Scaife, Austin, Texas; Rome
       Dennis E. Trout, Durham, North Carolina; Rome

# Appendix IV

## RECIPIENTS OF OVATIONES

1950 Clarence P. Bill
Norman J. DeWitt
Winifred G. Leutner
E. B. de Sauze
1951 Fred S. Dunham
Clyde Pharr
1952 Norman W. DeWitt
1953 None
1954 None
1955 Clyde Murley
Gertrude E. Smith
"the young teachers of Classics"
1956 Wilbert L. Carr
Russel M. Geer
1957 Lillian Gay Berry
A. Pelzer Wagener
Dorrance S. White
1958 Selatie E. Stout
B. L. Ullman
Harry J. Leon ("together with the staff of the Department of Classics at the University of Texas throughout its history")
1959 Walter R. Agard
Eleanore Cooper (of Scott Foresman and Company)
Irene J. Crabb
James E. Dunlap
1960 Annabel Horn
Donnis and Gladys Martin
1961 Charles C. Mierow
All the Editors of CJ
All the State Vice-Presidents of CAMWS
1962 Nellie Angel Smith
Herbert C. Youtie
1963 Alfred P. Dorjahn
Lillian B. Lawler
1964 John N. Hough
James J. Mertz, S.J.
Lucy A. Whitsel
1965 Grace L. Beede
Chauncey E. Finch

1966  D. Herbert Abel
      Graydon W. Regenos
1967  Clark Hopkins
      Margaret Forbes
      The Rev. Paul F. Distler
1968  William Korfmacher
      Sister Mary Bede Donelan
      Lucile Cox
1969  Paul R. Murphy
      Gertrude Ewing
      Margaret Smith
1970  Oscar E. Nybakken
      Edith M. Kovach
      Mary S. Duerson
1971  Clarence A. Forbes
      Gerald M. Erickson
      Vivia Craig
1972  William H. Willis
      Gertrude C. Drake
      Norman T. Pratt
1973  Gerald F. Else
      Eula G. Cutt
      James W. Alexander
1974  Paul Lachlan MacKendrick
      Richard Scanlan
      Ethel Poston
1975  Maurice P. Cunningham
      Waldo E. Sweet
      Elizabeth Hunter
1976  H. Lloyd Stow
      Annie Virginia Cook Aldridge
1977  Graves Haydon Thompson
      Geraldine Hodges
1978  Alexander Gordon McKay
      Bert Henry Narveson
      Kay de Pue
1979  Herbert W. Benario
      The Rev. Raymond V. Schoder
      Gerda Seligson
1980  Roger Allen Hornsby
      J. D. Sadler
      Ruth Froberg

1981  Harry C. Rutledge
      Gareth L. Schmeling
      Henrietta Davis
      Arthur F. Stocker
1982  Charles Luther Babcock
      Raymond L. Den Adel
      Christine Sleeper
1983  Kenneth J. Reckford
      Mark P. O. Morford
      Marcia McCathern Stille
1984  Gotthard Karl Galinsky
      Hunter Ripley Rawlings
      Jane H. Hall
1985  Brent M. Froberg
      Richard A. LaFleur
      Margaret Weaver
1986  Janice M. Benario
      Susan Ford Wiltshire
      Marian West Stocker
1987  Meyer Reinhold
      C. Wayne Tucker
      Dorothy Daniel
1988  J. Ward Jones
      Anna Lydia Motto
      Tamara Bauer

# *AppendixV*

## CAMWS ANNUAL MEETINGS

| | | |
|---|---|---|
| First | May 5, 6, 1905 | Chicago, Illinois |
| Second | May 4, 5, 1906 | Saint Louis, Missouri |
| Third | March 29, 30, 1907 | Chicago, Illinois |
| Fourth | April 17, 18, 1908 | Nashville, Tennessee |
| Fifth | February 24, 25, 1909 | New Orleans, Louisiana |
| Sixth | April 29, 30, 1910 | Chicago, Illinois |
| Seventh | April 7, 8, 1911 | St. Louis, Missouri |
| Eighth | April 12, 13, 1912 | Cincinnati, Ohio |
| Ninth | April 12, 13, 1913 | Indianapolis, Indiana |
| Tenth | April 10, 11, 1914 | Iowa City, Iowa |
| Eleventh | April 2, 3, 1915 | Nashville, Tennessee |
| Twelfth | April 21, 22, 1916 | Chicago, Illinois |
| Thirteenth | April 5, 6, 7, 1917 | Louisville, Kentucky |
| Fourteenth | April 4, 5, 6, 1918 | Omaha, Nebraska |
| Fifteenth | April 10, 11, 12, 1919 | Atlanta, Georgia |
| Sixteenth | April 1, 2, 3, 1920 | Cleveland, Ohio |
| Seventeenth | March 24, 25, 26, 1921 | Saint Louis, Missouri |
| Eighteenth | April 13, 14, 15, 1922 | Madison, Wisconsin |
| Nineteenth | March 29, 30, 31, 1923 | Columbia, Missouri |
| Twentieth | April 17, 18, 19, 1924 | Lexington, Kentucky |
| Twenty-first | April 9, 10, 11, 1925 | Iowa City, Iowa |
| Twenty-second | April 1, 2, 3, 1926 | Urbana, Illinois |
| Twenty-third | April 14, 15, 16, 1927 | Ann Arbor, Michigan |
| Twenty-fourth | April 5, 6, 7, 1928 | Nashville, Tennessee |
| Twenty-fifth | March 28, 29, 30, 1929 | Chicago, Illinois |
| Twenty-sixth | April 3, 4, 5, 1930 | New Orleans, Louisiana |
| Twenty-seventh | April 2, 3, 4, 1931 | Bloomington, Indiana |
| Twenty-eighth | March 24, 25, 26, 1932 | Cincinnati, Ohio |
| Twenty-ninth | April 13, 14, 15, 1933 | Williamsburg, Virginia |
| Thirtieth | March 29, 30, 31, 1934 | Memphis, Tennessee |
| Thirty-first | April 18, 19, 20, 1935 | Saint Louis, Missouri |
| Thirty-second | April 9, 10, 11, 1936 | Cleveland, Ohio |
| Thirty-third | March 25, 26, 27, 1937 | Nashville, Tennessee |
| Thirty-fourth | April 14, 15, 16, 1938 | Iowa City, Iowa |
| Thirty-fifth | April 6, 7, 8, 1939 | Oberlin, Ohio |
| Thirty-sixth | March 21, 22, 23, 1940 | Louisville, Kentucky |
| Thirty-seventh | April 10, 11, 12, 1941 | Indianapolis, Indiana |
| Thirty-eighth | April 2, 3, 4, 1942 | New Orleans, Louisiana |
| Thirty-ninth | April 22, 23, 24, 1943 | Chicago, Illinois |
| Fortieth | April 6, 7, 8, 1944 | Saint Louis, Missouri |
| Forty-first | March 29, 30, 31, 1945 | Cancelled |

| | | |
|---|---|---|
| Forty-second | April 18, 19, 20, 1946 | Cincinnati, Ohio |
| Forty-third | April 3, 4, 5, 1947 | Nashville, Tennessee |
| Forty-fourth | April 1, 2, 3, 1948 | Milwaukee, Wisconsin |
| Forty-fifth | April 7, 8, 9, 1949 | Richmond, Virginia |
| Forty-sixth | April 6, 7, 8, 1950 | Cleveland, Ohio |
| Forty-seventh | March 29, 30, 31, 1951 | Memphis, Tennessee |
| Forty-eighth | April 17, 18, 19, 1952 | Toronto, Ontario |
| Forty-ninth | April 2, 3, 4, 1953 | Cincinnati, Ohio |
| Fiftieth | April 22, 23, 24, 1954 | Saint Louis, Missouri |
| Fifty-first | April 7, 8, 9, 1955 | Chicago, Illinois |
| Fifty-second | April 5, 6, 7, 1956 | Lexington, Kentucky |
| Fifty-third | April 18, 19, 20, 1957 | Columbus, Ohio |
| Fifty-fourth | April 10, 11, 12, 1958 | Austin, Texas |
| Fifty-fifth | April 2, 3, 4, 1959 | Milwaukee, Wisconsin |
| Fifty-sixth | April 14, 15, 16, 1960 | Athens, Georgia |
| Fifty-seventh | April 6, 7, 8, 1961 | Cleveland, Ohio |
| Fifty-eighth | April 19, 20, 21, 1962 | Memphis, Tennessee |
| Fifty-ninth | April 18, 19, 20, 1963 | Chicago, Illinois |
| Sixtieth | March 26, 27, 28, 1964 | Charlottesville, Virginia |
| Sixty-first | April 22, 23, 24, 1965 | Toledo, Ohio |
| Sixty-second | April 7, 8, 9, 1966 | Norman, Oklahoma |
| Sixty-third | March 30, 31, April 1, 1967 | Indianapolis, Indiana |
| Sixty-fourth | April 11, 12, 13, 1968 | Atlanta, Georgia |
| Sixty-fifth | April 10, 11, 12, 1969 | Boulder, Colorado |
| Sixty-sixth | March 28, 29, 30, 1970 | Louisville, Kentucky |
| Sixty-seventh | April 1, 2, 3, 1971 | Minneapolis, Minnesota |
| Sixty-eighth | March 30, 31, April 1, 1972 | Durham, North Carolina |
| Sixty-ninth | April 12, 13, 14, 1973 | Detroit, Michigan |
| Seventieth | April 11, 12, 13, 1974 | New Orleans, Louisiana |
| Seventy-first | April 3, 4, 5, 1975 | Cleveland, Ohio |
| Seventy-second | April 15, 16, 17, 1976 | Knoxville, Tennessee |
| Seventy-third | April 7, 8, 9, 1977 | Iowa City, Iowa |
| Seventy-fourth | March 30, 31, April 1, 1978 | Houston, Texas |
| Seventy-fifth | April 19, 20, 21, 1979 | Madison, Wisconsin |
| Seventy-sixth | March 27, 28, 29, 1980 | Columbia, South Carolina |
| Seventy-seventh | April 16, 17, 18, 1981 | St. Louis, Missouri |
| Seventy-eighth | April 15, 16, 17, 1982 | Atlanta, Georgia |
| Seventy-ninth | April 7, 8, 9, 1983 | Columbus, Ohio |
| Eightieth | April 26, 27, 28, 1984 | Williamsburg, Virginia |
| Eighty-first | April 11, 12, 13, 1985 | Minneapolis, Minnesota |
| Eighty-second | April 17, 18, 19, 1986 | Tampa, Florida |
| Eighty-third | April 23, 24, 25, 1987 | Boulder, Colorado |
| Eighty-fourth | April 7, 8, 9, 1988 | New Orleans, Louisiana |

# Appendix VI

## CONSTITUTIONS OF THE ASSOCIATION

*The original, May 5, 1905*

### ARTICLE I

#### NAME AND OBJECT OF THE ASSOCIATION

SECTION I. This organization shall be known as the Classical Association of the Middle West and South. Its object shall be the advancement of classical learning, the encouragement of classical studies within the territory indicated, and the promotion of the common interests of its members through its meetings and publications.

### ARTICLE II

#### OFFICERS

SECTION I. The officers shall be a President; a number of Vice-Presidents, to correspond with the number of states participating in the Association, one to be chosen from each state; of these vice-presidents one shall be designated as First Vice-President, to preside in the absence of the President, and to succeed him in the event of a vacancy in that office; and a Secretary-Treasurer.

SEC. 2. There shall be an Executive Committee, consisting of the President, the First Vice-President, the Secretary-Treasurer, and four additional members to be elected by the Association. Of these four additional members, one shall at the first election be named for a term of four years, one for a term of three years, one for a term of two years, and one for a term of one year. Thereafter one member shall be elected annually to serve for a period of four years.

SEC. 3. There shall be a program committee constituted according to the provisions of Article V.

SEC. 4. The election of officers shall take place at the second business session of each regular annual meeting.

### ARTICLE III

#### MEETINGS

SECTION I. There shall be a regular annual meeting at such time and place as the Association at a preceding meeting shall have named.

SEC. 2. The arrangements for all meetings shall be under the general direction of the Executive Committee.

SEC. 3. Special meetings of the Association may be held at the call of the Executive Committee, at such time and place as they may determine.

# ARTICLE IV

## MEMBERSHIP

SECTION I. Any person resident within the territory designated by the name of the Association and approved by the Executive Committee may become a member on payment of the annual dues for the current fiscal year.

SEC. 2. The annual dues for each member shall be two dollars. Membership in the Association may be terminated if the annual dues of any member remain unpaid.

# ARTICLE V

## PROGRAM

The program of papers and addresses to be presented at the meetings of the Association shall be arranged by a committee which shall consist of the President, the Secretary-Treasurer, and a third member to be appointed by them. The President of the Association shall act as chairman of this committee.

# ARTICLE VI

## PUBLICATIONS

All publications of the Association, with the exception of announcements etc., shall be under the charge of a board of editors, to be appointed by the Executive Committee.

# ARTICLE VII

## AMENDMENTS

Changes in the above Constitution may be made by a two-thirds vote of the members present at a regular meeting, when written note of such change has been made at the regular meeting prceding, and has been deposited with the Secretary-Treasurer.

*The current version, April 28, 1984*

# ARTICLE I

## NAME AND OBJECT

SECTION 1. The name of this organization shall be "The Classical Association of the Middle West and South." Its territory shall embrace the thirty states included in the Middle West and South, Ontario, Manitoba, and such other provinces of Canada as may subsequently express a desire to affiliate with this organization.

SECTION 2. Its object shall be the advancement of classical scholarship, teaching, and appreciation, and the promotion of the common interests of its members through meetings, publications and like activities.

# ARTICLE II

## OFFICERS

SECTION 1. The officers shall be a President; a President-Elect; a first Vice-President, who will succeed to the presidency in case of a vacancy within that office and who will perform the functions of the President in case of the President's inability to act; local Vice-Presidents corresponding in number to the state or like political divisions participating in the Association; and a Secretary-Treasurer.

SECTION 2. The President, the President-Elect, and the first Vice-President shall serve for a term of one year, and shall not be eligible to succeed themselves immediately, but the President-Elect of each year shall automatically become the President for the following year. The Secretary-Treasurer, whose office shall be executive in character, shall serve for a term of one year, and shall be able to succeed himself (or herself) directly. The local Vice-Presidents shall serve for a term of two years, being elected in the even numbered years, and shall be eligible to succeed themselves immediately on recommendation of the Executive Committee.

SECTION 3. The Executive Committee shall have the power to fill vacancies occurring among the officers or within its own membership between Annual Business Meetings, except that (cf. Article II, Section 1, above) the first Vice-President shall automatically become President, if at any time the office of President becomes vacant. All such appointments shall be deemed to be interim in character, the appointee to serve only until the time of the next Annual Business Meeting, but persons so appointed to any office shall be eligible to succeed themselves directly by election at the next Annual Business Meeting. A President-Elect so designated by interim action of the Executive Committee shall not accede automatically the next year to the office of President, but his or her name shall automatically be placed in nomination for election to that office at the next Annual Business Meeting.

SECTION 4. There shall be an Executive Committee consisting of the President, the President-Elect, the first Vice-President, the Secretary-Treasurer, the immediate past President, the Editor of *The Classical Journal*, and four additional persons, who shall serve for terms of four years each, one term expiring each year.

In the event that the immediate past President is unable to serve because of death, incapacity, or removal from the area of the Association, his or her place on the Executive Committee shall be left vacant, and shall not be filled by the procedure described in Article II, Section 3, above.

SECTION 5. The President shall appoint, early in his or her year of office, a Nominating Committee, whose duty it shall be to propose a slate of officers to be elected at the next Annual Business Meeting, except that local Vice-Presidents shall be proposed for election by the Executive Committee.

SECTION 6. The duties of the officers of the Association shall be those which normally devolve upon such officials, except as provided in this instrument. Further definition of these duties shall be within the powers of the Executive Committee.

SECTION 7. The term of office for all officers shall begin on May 1 following the Annual Business Meeting. On July 1 the fiscal year of the Association shall begin.

SECTION 8. The Finance Committee of the Classical Association of the Middle West and South, Inc. shall have the authority and responsibility to manage the Association's investments. It shall report its activities annually to the Executive Board at its meeting before each annual convention of the Association.

The Finance Committee shall consist of three members including a chairperson appointed by the President for six-year terms. Initial terms shall be for two, four, and six years. Each subsequent appointment shall be for six years. The Chairperson of the Committee shall serve as a member of the Executive Board. The Secretary-Treasurer will be an ex-officio member of the Committee.

## ARTICLE III

### MEMBERSHIP

SECTION 1. Any person resident within the territory of the Association may become a member on payment of the annual dues for the current fiscal year.

SECTION 2. The annual membership fee shall be as from time to time determined at the Annual Business Meeting, and shall include a subscription to *The Classical Journal* or, when reciprocal arrangements with some other Association are in effect, a subscription to the journal of the Association. The Executive Committee may, in its discretion, set combination rates which will include membership in the Association and subscription to more than one journal, at a saving to the individual subscriber.

SECTION 3. Persons who have been members of the Association for as many as thirty years and who have retired from professional activity may upon payment of a prescribed fee, assume emeritus status. This fee shall be payable only once, and shall entitle the individual to life membership in the Association and receipt of its publications. The amount of the fee shall be as may from time to time be determined at the Annual Business Meeting.

## ARTICLE IV

### MEETINGS

SECTION 1. There shall normally be a regular Annual Meeting, including the Annual Business Meeting, at such time and place as the Association shall have determined at a previous Annual Business Meeting.

If, however, under exceptional circumstances, conditions appear to the Executive Committee to be such as to render the holding of the Annual Meeting impracticable or undesirable, the Executive Committee shall have the power to cancel the meeting, and itself to transact all business that would come before the Annual Business Meeting except the adoption of amendments to this Constitution and the election of new officers. The terms of all officers shall automatically be extended until the time of holding the next Business Meeting and the Executive Committee shall have the power to fill such vacancies as may occur in the roster of officers (Article II, Section 1, above) and in its own membership (Article II, Section 4, above), persons so chosen retaining their eligibility to succeed themselves directly by election at the next Business Meeting. The name of a President-Elect so chosen shall automatically be placed in nomination for election to the office of President at the next Business Meeting.

## ARTICLE V

### PROGRAM

The program of papers, addresses, and like events to be presented at the Annual Meeting shall be arranged by the President. Those presenting papers and residing within the territory of the Association must be members of the Association.

## ARTICLE VI

### PUBLICATIONS

Major publications of the Association, including *The Classical Journal*, shall be governed by a Board of Editors, among whom there shall be an Editor-In-Chief. The Editor-In-Chief shall be appointed (after an open search) by the Executive Committee, subject to the approval of the next

Annual Business Meeting, and shall be reviewed annually by the Executive Committee.

When a vacancy for Editor-In-Chief occurs, the President, with the approval of the Executive Committee, shall establish a search committee which will announce the availability of the position, receive nominations and applications, and conduct interviews with the finalists for the position. The search committee shall present its report and recommendations to the President and the Executive Committee. Other members of the Board of Editors shall be named by the Editor-In-Chief, subject to the approval of the Executive Committee.

## ARTICLE VII

### AMENDMENT

This Constitution may be revised or amended by a two-thirds vote of the members present and voting at any Annual Business Meeting, provided that the membership has been appraised of the substance of all revisions or amendments to be offered at least thirty days before the time of the meeting at which action is to be taken.

An amendment approved on April 9, 1988, increases the membership of the Executive Committee by inserting the following, after "the Editor of *The Classical Journal*," "the Chairpersons of the Committee for the Promotion of Latin and the Steering Committee on Awards and Scholarships,"

# Appendix VII

SELECT BIBLIOGRAPHY

W. R. Agard, "Classical Scholarship," in M. Curti, editor, *American Scholarship in the twentieth century* (Cambridge, MA, 1953) 146-167.

W. M. Calder III, "Die Geschichte der klassischen Philologie in den Vereinigten Staaten," *Jahrbuch für Amerikastudien* 11 (1966) 213-240 = *Studies in the Modern History of Classical Scholarship* (Naples 1984) 15-42.

W. L. Carr, "Our Association–The First Fifty Years," *CJ* 50 (1954-55) 195-199

F. W. Kelsey, "Latin in the High School," *Educational Review* 8 (1894) 25-42.

G. A. Kennedy, "Afterword: An Essay on Classics in America since the Yale Report," in M. Reinhold, *Classica Americana* (Detroit 1984) 325-351.

R. A. LaFleur, editor, *The Teaching of Latin in American Schools: A Profession in Crisis* (Atlanta 1987).

P. MacKendrick, "The Next Fifty Years," *CJ* 50 (1954-55) 201-204.

F. G. Moore, "A History of the American Philological Association," *TAPA* 50 (1919) 5-32.

C. Murley, "Dicenda Tacenda," *CJ* 50 (1954-55) 200.

M. Reinhold, "The Silver Age of Classical Studies in America, 1790-1830," *Classica Americana* (Detroit 1984) 174-203.

M. Reinhold, "The Latin Tradition in America," *Helios* 14 (1987) 123-139.

L. R. Shero, *The American Philological Association. An Historical Sketch* (Philadelphia 1964) = *TAPA* 94 (1963) x-1.

P. Shorey, "Fifty Years of Classical Studies in America," *TAPA* 50 (1919) 33-61.

P. Shorey, "The Case for the Classics," in F. W. Kelsey, editor, *Latin and Greek in American Education* (New York 1927²) 249-314.

E. Sihler, "Klassische Studien und klassischer Unterricht in den Vereinigten Staaten," *Neue Jahrbücher für das klassische Altertum, Geschichte und deutsche Literatur und für Pädagogik* 10 (1902) 458-463, 503-516, 548-556.

G. H. Thompson, *A History of the Southern Section of the Classical Association of the Middle West and South* (Athens, GA 1980).

A. F. West et al, *The Classical Investigation* (Princeton 1924 and 1925).